MW00653276

SECRETS OF OLD DARTMOUTH

By

Kathleen Ryan Comiskey Roberts

ILLUSTRATORS

Lelah Billington
Nancy Lundy
Preston Cook, Jr.
Jane Nicholson
Eric Greene
Carol Portnoy
Suanne Grove
Gilbert Rapoza
Cynthia King
Gina Sherman
Michael Travers

Seventh Grade Pupils
Mary A. Crapo School
1959–1960

1963 Original Edition
1976 Revised Edition
2010 Second Edition

Published by Vineyard Sound Books
370 Fisher Road
Dartmouth, MA 02747
www.VineyardSoundBooks.com

Printed in the United States of America

Edited by Lynn B. Pugh

Graphics by Monica Ann Luzzo-Moyer

Back cover photo by Christina Styan, The Chronicle, Dartmouth, MA.

Library of Congress Cataloging-in-Publication Data

Roberts, Kathleen Ryan Comiskey, 1914-
Secrets of Old Dartmouth / Kathleen Ryan Comiskey Roberts

Education / United States History
ISBN: 978-0-9825075-5-1

Printed in the United States by:
BookMasters, Inc.
30 Amberwood Parkway, Ashland, OH 44805
December 2010, M8046

IN LOVING MEMORY OF MY PARENTS,
ANN WHELAN RYAN AND THOMAS J. RYAN, SR.,
WHO LOVED CHILDREN, STORIES, AND DARTMOUTH.

Dear Boys and Girls,

This history of Dartmouth was written especially for you in order that you can learn more about your town. As you read this book, think of what life was like for the children who lived in your town years ago.

May you have as much pleasure reading these stories as I had writing them for you.

~ K.R.C.R.

TABLE OF CONTENTS

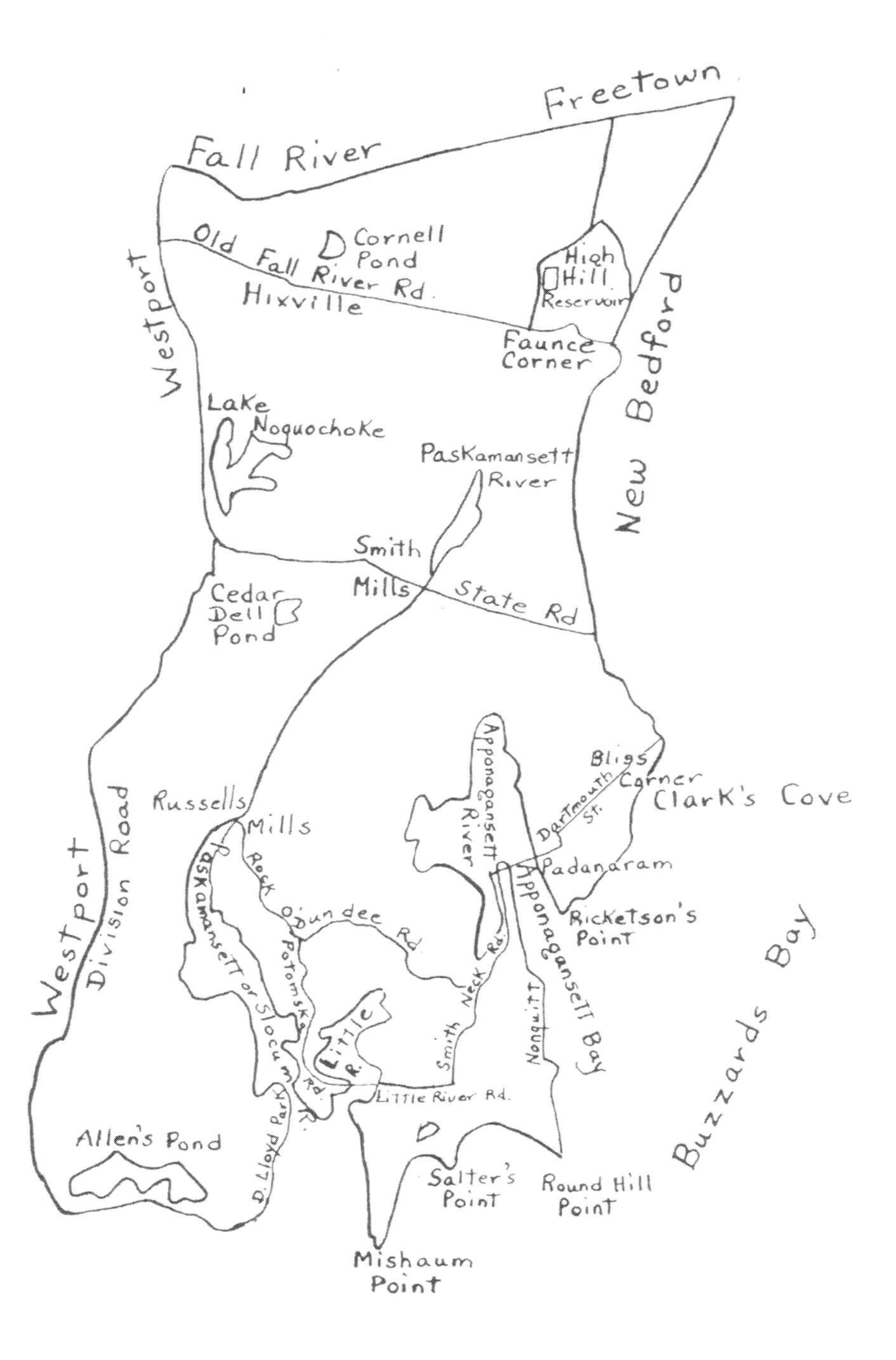

Dartmouth is the fourth largest town in area in Massachusetts.

CHAPTER 1

DARTMOUTH'S FIRST INHABITANTS

Who were the first inhabitants of Dartmouth? The first people who lived in our town were not white people.

Dartmouth's first inhabitants were Native American tribesmen. Dartmouth belonged to them for hundreds of years before the white people settled here.

When someone uses the word "Native Americans," what comes to your mind?

As you read this story, you may be surprised at how much we learned from the Native American people, the First Americans. The Pilgrims who landed in Plymouth in 1620 probably could not have survived without the help of the Native Americans.

Dartmouth's Native Americans were the Acushnets, the Apponegansets, and the Acoaxets, all members of the Wampanoag Tribe. The Wampanoags belonged to the once powerful Algonquin Native American tribe who claimed New England as their territory. These Native Americans loved to roam freely through the woods. Dartmouth was one of their village areas. They must have enjoyed Dartmouth, for much of it was wooded at that time. Dartmouth's nearness to water, both fresh and salt, was another reason the Native Americans liked Dartmouth. They were attracted to Dartmouth by the abundance of both fresh and salt water. Fresh water is necessary for human life. Fresh and salt water are means of transportation and sources of food and trading.

What was Dartmouth like then? Dartmouth was a wilderness. Remember, there were no stores or shops in the wilderness; there was no place one could go to buy things. The Native people had to be able to take care of their own needs. It is absolutely necessary that all people have food, clothing, and shelter. To secure their food, clothing, shelter, and also their tools and utensils, the Wampanoags learned to make use of the plants and animals that were around them. For a few items, such as copper, they did some trading with neighboring tribes, but mostly they hunted, fished, and raised food.

FOOD

When they were hungry, what did the Native Americans have for food? Where did they get it? They ate the plants, animals, and fish they found around them. They also planted seeds. The food the Wampanoags ate came from the ocean, rivers, woods, marshes, and fields near home. Unlike us, they did not eat three meals a day. They ate only when they were hungry. Indeed, sometimes they would go several days without much food, but generally speaking, they ate once a day around noon.

Since the Native Americans had no cows or goats, the children did not have milk to drink as you do. Water was their drink. The sassafras tree, which grew in abundance — and still grows here — was used to make a sassafras tea, which the adults drank. The Native Americans never could have bacon for breakfast or a ham sandwich for lunch because they did not have any pigs. Neither did they have sheep. The only domesticated animal they had was the dog. All the other animals mentioned were brought to our country later by the white men. But turkeys, described by the early settlers as "… of an incredible bigness …," were abundant.

The sea supplied the Dartmouth Native Americans with much food. Ponds and rivers also offered them food, for they were alive with fish. Two of these rivers are the Acushnet River, which flows into Buzzard's Bay at the present city of New Bedford, and the Apponegansett River, which has Padanaram Harbor as its mouth. The Little River, and the Slocum River, which empty into Buzzard's Bay at Potomska (South Dartmouth), also helped to supply the Wampanoags with food. So did the Westport River.

Many kinds of fish, such as eels, scup, cod, mackerel, bluefish, smelt, herring, tautog, and shad contributed to the Native American diet. The area also abounded in shellfish, such as clams, quahogs, mussels, periwinkles, scallops, oysters, crabs, and lobsters. Sometimes they might eat their shellfish raw, or would steam, boil, or roast them as we do at a clambake today.

Rivers, streams, and swamps also provided an abundance of waterfowl. Pheasants, partridges, and quails were trapped.

Often the Native Americans fished at night by torchlight. In the fresh water ponds in this area, they usually speared pickerel and pike.

To help them catch fish, the Native Americans made fish traps. For bait fishing, they used a gorge as their fishhook. A gorge was a straight, narrow piece of bone about an inch long, sharpened at both ends. The fish line was tied at the midpoint of the gorge. The baited gorge was swallowed whole by the fish. As the bait came off the gorge into the fish's mouth, the gorge then went crosswise in the fish's throat. The fisher who was holding onto the line could feel the fish's pull, and would haul the line in.

Have you ever eaten eels? They are delicious when fried. The Native Americans ate eels. They had a way of catching them by treading the eels out of the river mud with their feet and scooping them up with their hands or baskets. The women skinned the eels with their stone knives, then cleaned and prepared them for cooking. After that, the eels were smoked slowly as they hung over an outside fire. Smoking preserves fish, meat, and poultry. Nowadays, if we need extra vitamins we can buy vitamin pills. The Wampanoags got some of their vitamins from the oil in the eels.

In the spring, eels leave the shallower waters near the shore and go out to sea. The Wampanoag men built weirs across streams. Consequently, the eels and other fish were forced to swim through the narrow opening of the weir. Here it was fairly easy for the men to catch the fish.

Sometimes the Native Americans used dugouts—which they obtained by trade from northern Native Americans—when spearing for fish or lobsters. Often they walked into the water to spear lobsters that were close to the shore. The Native Americans did not mind walking into the water because they were strong swimmers. Their spears, used in lobstering, were long two-pronged forks. They were made of wood with the tips fire-hardened.

In New Bedford, there is a little point of land facing the Acushnet River. This piece of land was once called "Smoking Rock." The Wampanoags used to gather there for clambakes. How do we know they held clambakes at this spot? When the land there was plowed over by the white settlers, heaps of discarded clamshells were found. Mingled among them were stone knives, stone arrowheads, and bits of bones from the fishhooks. Does this help you to understand how clambakes, so common here in the summertime, had their origin?

FARMING

Although Dartmouth's soil was stony and not very rich, the First Americans farmed here. Indeed, they were good farmers. They cleared the land by cutting down large trees. They put a thick ring of wet clay around the tree trunk about two feet up from the ground. Then they lit a fire all the way around the base of each tree. They kept the clay wet and this fire burning until it had burned far enough through the tree from all sides so that the tree toppled over. Only the stumps were left.

Native American women planted all the crops except for tobacco, which was planted by the men. The Native American farmers planted their crops between the stumps of the trees. They planted seeds and raised corn, several varieties of beans, pumpkins, squash, cucumbers, and tobacco.

Native American using fish for fertilizer.

Corn was their chief food, summer and winter. The Native Americans had a clever way of deciding when to plant their corn. They said, "When the oak leaf has uncurled to the size of a mouse's ear, it is time to plant our corn." They used a stone hoe or maybe just a pointed stick. A stick of wood was used for making holes in the ground. You might say it served as a rake-hoe. Sometimes crude hoes were made by fastening a large clam or quahog shell to a stick. Deer antlers were sometimes used this way, too. The antlers were used to rake over the ground in the field. Sometimes the fields were raked over with scrapers made of shells and chipped stone (flint).

For fertilizer, in order to make the soil richer, they used fish and kelp (seaweed). The fish and kelp was buried in the soil with the seeds. The Native Americans dropped a fish or two in every little hill of seed to help the plant grow tall and strong. Then they watched their fields closely for a while after planting. Do you know why they did this? This was done to keep the wild animals from digging up the fish.

When we plant seeds now we sometimes use scarecrows to keep birds away from the seeds. It was the duty of the Native American women and children to drive off the flocks of hungry birds that came to eat the seed.

The tobacco raised by Native American men was used for smoking in pipes that they made from wood or clay found in the area. Their pipes were called calumets.

BERRYING

Another chore of the women and children was to gather the food that could be found in the woods. Wild fruits were quite plentiful. Blueberries, huckleberries, blackberries, raspberries, grapes, strawberries, beach plums, and cranberries all grew in Dartmouth. Cranberries grow in swamp areas, as they need much water. How many of these wild fruits have you picked?

Naturally, some of the berries were eaten right away, but many of the berries were dried for future use. When they were dried, they were put into sturdy baskets woven of reeds and rushes found along the shores of the ponds. Then these baskets of berries were placed in shallow holes in the ground for use in the winter.

USE OF NUTS, ROOTS, AND HERBS

The Wampanoags ate the nuts that grew here. The most common of these nuts were walnuts, hazelnuts, chestnuts, hickory nuts, and acorns. According to Roger Williams, one of the founding fathers of Rhode Island, a favorite dish was stewed acorns. An English author named Mourt who came to America in the sixteen hundreds gave us this information about acorns:

"Akornes also they (referring to the Native American people) dry, and in case of want of Corne, by much boyling they make a good dish of them: yea sometimes in plentie of Corne doe they eat these acornes for a noveltie."

Mourt also said, "Two baskets of parched acorns hidden in the ground which we supposed had been Corne when we baganne to digge the same."

The Native Americans knew the wild roots that were edible. In spring and summer, they went searching for fresh green herbs that were good to eat or those which could be used for medicinal purposes.

The Native American people were extremely helpful to the early settlers in Plymouth, identifying those plants that could be safely eaten. Of the small wild onions found here the settlers said, (they) "... eate well in sallet (salad) or baked meat."

DRIED FOODS

Drying preserves food. Besides drying berries, the Native American women also dried corn, squash, meat, and fish.

Dried corn was their grain food for the winter. Much of the corn was crushed or pounded into meal by the women. That was hard work. How did they do it?

Sometimes the dry kernels of corn were placed on a large, flat stone in the center of which had been made a shallow depression like a saucer. Then the Native American woman would crush them with another smaller stone she could handle easily.

Also used was a mortar and a pestle. The mortar might be called a bowl. It was hewn out of rock by chipping, scraping, and rubbing. The pestle was another rock used as a pounder. It was slightly rounded by the same method of chipping, scraping, and rubbing. After much use, the mortar and pestle became smooth. Can you understand why these were among the cherished possessions of the Native American women?

Corn was also used to make bread and pudding. Native American pudding made from corn meal is a dessert people in this area enjoy. Have you ever eaten it?

WHAT NATIVE AMERICANS OBTAINED FROM THE WOODS

The woodlands of Dartmouth were filled with many wild animals which provided meat for the Wampanoags. These Native Americans knew the woods well. They hunted and killed the animals with bows and arrows, traps, snares, knives, spears, and clubs.

Wild turkeys were found in abundance in the forests. The Native Americans ate many turkeys and other wild birds. Sometimes they ate the birds' eggs.

Deer were one of the most plentiful animals. Have you ever seen a deer here? Sometimes these graceful animals can be seen at a distance in the meadows of Dartmouth. They are beautiful creatures. In many respects, the deer took the place of the cow. The Wampanoags used the flesh for food. The hide was used for moccasins, other clothing, and blankets. The deer antlers were used to scrape and plow the ground.

There were small bears native to this area. They also provided food for the First Americans. Their hides were used for blankets and capes. The Wampanoags smeared bear grease on their bodies as an insect repellent, and it was also used to keep their skin soft. Bear grease was also used for frying food. A white lady, Mary Rowlandson, who was captured and lived a long time with a Native American tribe in central Massachusetts, wrote this in her diary:

"Afterwards, he (the sachem) asked me to make a cap for his boy for which he invited me to dinner. I went: and he gave me a pancake about as big as two fingers: it was made of parched wheat, beaten and fried in bear's grease: but I thought I never tasted pleasanter meat in my life."

Nowadays, turtle soup is considered a delicacy. The First Americans ate turtles. It may seem strange to you to learn that they also ate skunk. They knew how to remove its perfume sac. Skunk oil was considered a cure for pneumonia and other ills.

The Wampanoags ate partridges, ducks, pheasants, geese, coots, and heron. Muskrats, squirrels, rabbits, weasels, mink, fox, and beaver were taken not only for their furs, but for food as well. You probably have not seen a beaver here, but partridges, ducks, rabbits, and pheasants still provide beauty and food to Dartmouth.

There were sugar maple trees in Old Dartmouth. The Native Americans knew how to boil down the sap and use it as a sweetener. They especially liked it with corn.

TOOLS

Today, many of the tools we use are made of iron or steel. The Native Americans used shells, stones, or the bones and antlers of animals for cutting tools. Scrapers were made out of shells or chipped stones. Awls were made from the large bones of the larger animals they killed. Hammers, mallets, and hatchets were made by attaching a stone to a sturdy stick with thongs.

Most utensils used by the Native people were made of wood or the bark of trees.

CLOTHING

How did the Native Americans dress? They used the skins of animals for clothes. It was hard work to make their clothes. Sewing was not easy. The animal hides were scraped and cut with knives and scrapers by the women.

The women usually wore a one-piece deerskin wrap-around skirt and a jacket. The men frequently wore nothing above their waists. For special ceremonies, the women dressed in long one-piece garments which they had painted or decorated beautifully with animal hair, shells, porcupine quills, or bird feathers. The men's shirts were similarly decorated. These garments were fringed. The fringe made it more attractive and it saved sewing.

Both sexes wore moccasins made from deerskin.

In colder weather, the women wore long dresses. The men wore leggings, and armbands were sometimes worn as well. In the winter, they used animal skin robes which left one shoulder uncovered. These robes or mantles were called blankets.

MONEY

Do you know what the Native Americans used for money? They used wampum as we use money. They made wampum from shells. What kind of shells do you think they used for wampum? Did you guess clamshells? They usually used hard clamshells. We call the hard clam a quahog.

The First Americans did not use the quahog shells just as they found them. First, they broke or cut the shells. Then they took the small pieces of quahog shells and polished them by rubbing them in very fine sand. A hole was bored through the middle of the shell. The money was strung like beads on a thong made of animal skin.

JEWELRY

From very early times, people have worn jewelry or decorations. The Native Americans were no exception. They wore beads made from wampum, colored stones such as quartz, seeds, and nuts such as acorns and horse chestnuts. They used the burr, as well as the horse chestnut itself. Indeed, whatever nut they had they would use. They frequently wore copper obtained by trading with other Native American tribes farther west.

As ornaments, turkey feathers and shells were tucked into their hair. In particular, turkey feathers were highly valued for ornaments. Porcupine quills were also worn.

Do you know what a pendant is? This kind of jewelry was frequently worn by the Wampanoags. Pendants were made from shells, stones, or animals' teeth. They also used the paws of small animals such as beaver, squirrel, muskrat, rabbit, and skunk. Even now some people consider wearing a paw pendant or hanging one in a car window a sign of good luck. This custom was derived from contact with the Native Americans.

Some of the Native Americans wore bands of wampum around their foreheads. Others placed a band of wampum around their necks. This served as a necklace or a collar. On rare occasions, some of the sachems (chiefs) had acquired wampum belts that reached below the knee. Wampum beads were also made into bracelets. Today, wampum jewelry is very popular with both men and women.

HOMES

The Wampanoag home, which was called a wetu, (was frequently called a wigwam) was circular in shape at the base. It was made of bark or mats or even of skins spread over a framework of poles. A space was left for a door. In the center of the wetu was a stone hearth upon which a fire was built. The smoke could go out through the hole that was formed where the poles came together at the top of the wetu.

A number of wetus placed fairly close together made up a village. The Wampanoags usually lived in villages. There were several villages in Old Dartmouth.

The Native Americans hung their bows, arrows, cases, and tools on hooks made of deer antlers or crotch sticks. These were tied with thongs to the poles supporting the wetu.

What did the Native Americans use for their beds? Sometimes they slept on skins or finely woven mats spread on the ground, but mostly the skins were placed over a platform not very high off the floor.

Also in the wetu were large baskets that had been woven by the women. These were used for storage.

If there was a baby in the family, at night they hung the cradleboard, baby and all, on one of the hooks.

In the winter, the Wampanoags dug holes in the floor of wetu in which to store food. They would dig in the soil and bury the food: corn, nuts, dried fish, and meat for the winter. These stored foods were in addition to the supplies placed in root cellars dug in the hills. These were very necessary when the weather was inclement so they would not have to leave their home. Can you picture what it was like to live in a wetu?

TRANSPORTATION

How did the Native Americans get from one place to another in this wilderness? Usually they walked. By following the same route, over and over again, trails were developed. These trails often followed the trails made by animals. The animal trails went to places where water could be found. The Wampanoags needed trails for hunting, trading, to get water, and for transportation. Some roads in present-day Dartmouth were once the trails of the First Americans. These include Slocum Road, Tucker Road, Chase Road, and Barney's Joy Road. Of course, when cars were developed, trails had to be widened and in some places straightened out.

In all seasons but winter the rivers and the ocean were the principal roadways. The Native Americans traveled along the water in the dugouts they had obtained by trade with northern Native Americans. The Native Americans also made canoes covered with birch bark and used them to travel from place to place.

It was hard work to make a canoe. Both men and women worked on it. The men gathered the materials. The women did much of the work putting them together. Most of the canoes held one or two men and were about eighteen feet long. They were light enough to be carried, when necessary, by one man. Some canoes were as long as forty feet. Ten paddlers were needed for these long canoes. They were usually war canoes.

The framework of the canoe was made of cedar, willow, ash, and other woods that bend easily into shape. The smaller branches of these woods were used. They were tied together with sinews taken from the tendons of animals and thongs made from the skins of animals cut into strips. This framework was covered with the bark from a birch tree. It was made waterproof with the tar or pitch from the pine, hemlock, or spruce tree.

The women sewed the sections of the canoe together. First, using a bone awl they cut the holes. Rootlets of trees (the tiny roots) were used for thread.

The paddles we use today are modeled after the paddles used by the First Americans. Canoes then did not have seats. When paddling, the Native Americans would kneel on the bottom of the canoe, usually on a pad made from a folded deerskin.

In addition to making birch bark canoes, the Native Americans also made dugouts for traveling on the water. First, a large tree was cut down. It was hard work to cut down trees. The First Americans did not have the tools we have now. To fell the tree for a canoe, they would burn through part of the tree just above the ground. They would put wet clay just above the burning section so the fire would not spread upward. Once the tree was felled, the inside of the log was burned out gradually. A small section would be burned. Then the fire was put out with water and the charred wood scraped out. This process was repeated many times until the desired shape for the inside of the dugout was finally achieved.

In winter, the Wampanoags used toboggans for carrying heavy loads. They also used sleds for pulling loads over snow and ice. When the snow was fresh on the ground, sometimes they would travel on snowshoes. Indeed, the Native Americans invented snowshoes. For winter travel, they used snowshoes to walk on top of the deep drifts without getting their feet wet. They made their snowshoes from a flat frame of wood, three of four feet long and about one-third as wide. (Snowshoes for women were smaller.) The holder for the person's foot rested on the woven section of the snowshoe, which was made out of thongs from hides and skin. When the Native American wore snowshoes, he could walk on snowdrifts without sinking.

The women did not carry their babies in their arms. Instead, while working or traveling, they carried their babies in a cradleboard on their backs. While working in the gardens, the mothers would hang the cradleboards on the branch of a tree.

Thus, the babies could sleep while the mothers worked or moved about.

OUR HERITAGE FROM THE NATIVE AMERICANS

The First Americans taught us many things. From them we learned about the native foods that were good to eat. They taught us how to hunt, trap, fish, and farm here. We adopted their idea of snowshoes for winter travel. We added Native American words such as moccasins, wetu, skunk, Yankee, succotash, woodchuck, beans, and peas to our vocabulary. We adopted their names for places such as Apponeganset, Cuttyhunk, and Massachusetts. From them we learned how to make canoes. They taught us how to tap maple trees to get the syrup. From them we learned how to fish through the ice.

White people in America owe much to the earliest inhabitants of this land, the Native Americans.

CHAPTER 2

DARTMOUTH'S FIRST WHITE VISITOR

Have you ever dreamed of being an explorer and going to a place where no civilized man has ever been? How do you think the first white man to set foot on the Native American territory of Dartmouth felt? The first white visitor to ever come here gave us a good picture of Dartmouth as it was over three and one half centuries ago.

Who was the first white man to come to Dartmouth? Where did he come from?

According to the old Norse sagas (stories) and Native American legends, Eric the Red sailed into Buzzard's Bay in the tenth century. Norse refers to Norway where the Vikings first lived. Norway is a country across the Atlantic Ocean in Northern Europe.

If Eric the Red did sail into Buzzard's Bay, he probably came to Dartmouth. But we cannot be certain because he left no proof of his visit. The Norsemen were also called Vikings. We are certain the Vikings did sail great distances from their homes in Greenland, Iceland, and Norway. We know they came to this part of the country. Since they failed to leave any records of their exploring, we cannot be absolutely sure they came to our town.

CAPTAIN BARTHOLOMEW GOSNOLD

However, we do have proof that, ever so many years ago in 1602, Captain Bartholomew Gosnold, a daring English adventurer, sailed across Buzzard's Bay and explored the area where we live. That makes Captain Gosnold the first white man ever to come to Dartmouth who kept a written record of his explorations. He sailed across the Atlantic Ocean from Falmouth, England to America.

Why did Gosnold come to America? He came for two reasons. Gosnold wanted to find a more direct and shorter course to our present-day America than the earlier explorers had used.

A Native American watches as Gosnold approaches the shore of Old Dartmouth.

He also expected to start a plantation somewhere along the Atlantic coastline. Before reaching our area, Captain Gosnold landed on Cape Cod. He named the cape "Cape Cod" because of the abundance of cod fish in the waters that wash the cape's shores. Gosnold wrote that he found an abundance of unripe strawberries on Cape Cod. He also commented that there was much sand and it was very deep. He was probably referring to the sand dunes. Gosnold wrote that he met friendly Native Americans. Another interesting thing he wrote was that one young Native American had plates of copper in his ears.

The name of Gosnold's ship was the Concord. The Concord's homeport was Dartmouth, England. Gosnold sailed from Dartmouth, England with a crew of thirty-one men. Gosnold stopped at what is now called Cuttyhunk Island. He gave this island the name "Elizabeth" in honor of the queen of England. Later the name Elizabeth was used to name all the islands from Nonamesett to Cuttyhunk. Cuttyhunk, the name given to one island by the Native Americans, was adopted by the white men. Cuttyhunk is the westernmost island of the Elizabeth Islands. If you haven't visited Cuttyhunk Island, you have probably seen it. On a clear day, this two and one half mile long island can be seen easily from Salter's Point, Mishaum Point, Smith Neck, or the Town Landing.

Gosnold must have meant to have some of his men remain in this area for some time because at Cuttyhunk he had his crew build a storehouse and a fort. The site of these was a small island in a fresh water pond. They also built a flat bottomed boat to get from the island to the shore of the pond. Gosnold said, while on Cuttyhunk, he and his crew "... feasted and grew fat on the young sea fowl they found in their nests."

GOSNOLD'S VISIT TO THE MAINLAND

Looking across from Cuttyhunk, Gosnold could see the mainland. Dartmouth was on the mainland directly across from Cuttyhunk. Gosnold decided to see what the mainland was like. While some of his men continued working at Cuttyhunk, Gosnold and others of his crew sailed across the bay and landed on the shore near Round Hill. Do you know where Round Hill is? It is on Smith Neck Road in South Dartmouth near Salter's Point. Maybe you have been swimming there, for now it is a town beach. Gosnold called Round Hill "Hap's Hill" because it was hoped "... much hap (happiness) might be expected from it."

While on this expedition to Dartmouth, Gosnold was met by a group of Native American men, women, and children. The Native American people were very friendly to Gosnold and his men although initially they were slow to approach the white people. Perhaps they were thinking of the ill treatment their people had received by some whites in earlier years.

Gosnold did some trading with the Native Americans. The Native Americans gave Gosnold tobacco, hemp, turtles, boiled fish in twig baskets, artificial strings, colored wampum, and the skins of such wild animals as deer, otter, fox, beaver, and wildcat. How pleased Gosnold was! The Native Americans also gave Gosnold some sassafras roots. Have you ever seen sassafras? You can still find it in Dartmouth. In Gosnold's time, sassafras was in great demand by whites. It was used as medicine as well as a drink. (Remember, the First Americans already used it to make tea.) Gosnold continued to explore that day, but as night approached, he returned to Cuttyhunk. Gosnold did all his exploring by daylight, but at night he always retuned to the fortress in the pond on the island of Cuttyhunk.

GOSNOLD'S DESCRIPTION

The captain had much praise for our locality. He described the Native Americans as "... a fair-conditioned people, gentle of disposition." What do you think he meant? He also said the Native Americans treated him and his men with "...all courteous kindness." That is fine praise. If company comes to your house and they say something like that about you, it makes your mother very happy.

Gosnold described the mainland thus, "The main the goodliest continent he had ever seen promising more by far than we did in any way expect, for it is replenished with fair fields and with fragrant flowers, also meadows, and hedged in with stately groves, being furnished also with pleasant brooks and beautified with two main rivers."

Remember that when Gosnold spoke of the mainland he meant Dartmouth. What do you suppose he meant when he said, "It is replenished with fair fields and with fragrant flowers?"

Dartmouth still has some beautiful meadows. Just before it is time to cut the hay, the meadows are colorful. Next summer stop and look at one of Dartmouth's meadows. They really are pretty.

Captain Gosnold mentioned our "stately groves." Do you know what groves are? At that time, there were groves of beech and cedar in our town. Are there any groves in Dartmouth now?

Gosnold said the mainland was "beautified with two main rivers." The two rivers spoken of by our first white visitor are the Acushnet River, which separates New Bedford and Fairhaven, and the Apponegansett River, which flows into the Padanaram Harbor. Gosnold made two other remarks that might interest you. While here, he picked some wild strawberries. Later he said they were, "… as sweet and much bigger than in England." Gosnold also mentioned that deer and other wild beasts were very plentiful. Thanks to Captain Gosnold, we have a better picture of Old Dartmouth.

GOSNOLD'S VISITORS

Remember, you read that Gosnold returned to Cuttyhunk Island. A few days later, while Gosnold's men were still working on their shelters on Cuttyhunk Island, they saw some canoes approaching. How surprised they were! The canoes were coming from Dartmouth. There were almost a dozen canoes. Who do you think was in these canoes? Fifty Native Americans were in the canoes. If forty-seven of them were men, how many women were there? Because Gosnold did not want the Native American people to discover his fortifications, he left the fort and went to meet them. He and some of his men met the natives at the shore. In Gosnold's words although the Native Americans acted very friendly they carried bows and arrows with them.

The purpose of the Native Americans' visit was to trade their furs for some goods from the white men. Gosnold said the Native Americans brought skins of beaver, martin, otter, wildcat, black fox, coney-skins, seal, and other skins not known to Gosnold and his men. Just think of all the wild animals found in Dartmouth then! In return for the furs, the white men gave straw hats and knives.

From Gosnold's records, we also learned that "The Native Americans brought boiled fish in baskets made of twigs." They smoked tobacco in clay and copper pipes. Three days were spent in trading on Cuttyhunk Island. Gosnold said most of the Native American people were dressed in deerskins. The men and the women dressed in about the same way and adorned themselves with feathers and copper beads. The explorer also mentioned that these Native American men were taller than the Englishmen, but the Native American women were short and fat.

The Native Americans sometimes ate with the white men. Gosnold tells us the Native Americans did not like the flavor of mustard. The English had also said a few of the Native American men had thin black beards, but most of them did not have beards. Strange as it may seem to us, some of the Native Americans had make-believe beards that were made from the hair of animals. It was the custom in those days for white men to grow beards. In his writings, Gosnold tells us that one Native American man wanted to trade his make-believe beard for the red beard of one of the white men. It was apparent that the Native American man did not think the white man's beard could be real because he had never seen a reddish-colored beard before. How the white men must have chuckled at that! Probably, they teased their companion about trading his "make-believe" beard.

Did you ever wonder how the First Americans made a fire since they had no matches? Gosnold reported that the Native Americans he saw had fire-making sets. These fire-making sets were carried in small leather bags. The leather bags, made from animal skins, were attached to a belt the Native American men wore around their waist. Gosnold tells us his men asked one of the Native American men to strike a fire. The Native American did so with an "emerald stone, such as glaziers."

The Native Americans did their trading with the white men in the daytime. As night approached, the Native Americans retired to the opposite end of Cuttyhunk. After three days of trading, the Native Americans got into their canoes and paddled back to the mainland.

GOSNOLD RETURNS TO ENGLAND

Gosnold and his men did not stay here very long. Originally, some of his crew were to remain in this area, but in the end, they all sailed away. Gosnold arrived here in May. In June, he sailed back to England to sell his cargo of sassafras, cedar trees, and furs.

Although Gosnold later returned to America, he did not come back to Dartmouth. He went instead to Virginia with the famous Captain John Smith. Gosnold was captain of the "God Speed," one of three ships that arrived in Jamestown, Virginia in 1607. Gosnold was also a member of the council that governed the Jamestown settlement. Gosnold did not live very long after arriving in Jamestown. He died in 1607; he is buried in Jamestown in an unmarked grave.

Just think, if Gosnold had established a successful colony here, Dartmouth, not Jamestown, would have been the first permanent English settlement in America!

CHAPTER 3

THE PURCHASE OF DARTMOUTH, 1652

When your mother sends you to the store to buy something, what do you have with you? Your answer is probably money, and is right, of course. This story is about a very large purchase paid for with — no— not money this time! If you read this story, you will find out what was used instead of money.

The earliest settlers in our Commonwealth of Massachusetts came from England. These courageous men and women formed colonies in Plymouth (1620), Salem (1628), and the Boston area (1630). Soon, some of these colonies wanted to spread out and gain new territory. Some were sent away from the early settlements, usually for religious reasons. A few of them moved to Dartmouth.

When did the settlers decide to come to this locality? We cannot be sure just when the first white person moved to Dartmouth. We do know that between 1630 and 1650 some people spread out into what was an unknown wilderness.

The first white people to make their homes in Dartmouth came from the Plymouth Colony. This is not strange since the boundary of Plymouth Colony almost reached Dartmouth.

Earlier, the Plymouth Colony had made peace with the Native American grand sachem (chief), Massasoit. Massasoit's real name was Wasamegin, meaning "Yellow Feather." He was described as a "... man of peace and integrity and excellence of character." Massasoit was a remarkable man. Truly, he was the best friend the English settlers ever had. The settlers in Plymouth Colony knew our section of Massachusetts belonged to Massasoit. They did not take the land as some settlers did. In some places, the early settlers to America just pushed the Native Americans from their land. But a small group of Plymouth settlers asked Massasoit to sell this land to them. Massasoit agreed to sell them the land.

Massasoit sells Dartmouth to the white people. Name some of the things pictured that were used as payment for the land. Were the berries mentioned?

PURCHASE PRICE

It is said that the white men bought the land from Massasoit. How much money do you think they paid for it? Actually, not much money was given for the land. Instead, the purchasers gave the Native Americans things they needed or wanted. Here is a list of commodities the Native Americans received in exchange for the land:

"30 yards of cloth
Eight moose skins
Fifteen hoes
Fifteen axes
Eight blankets
Two kettles
One cloak
Two English pounds in wampum
Eight pairs of shoes
One iron pot
Ten shillings in another comodite"

Does this list seem a little strange to you? We certainly don't buy land that way now. But that was the way the earliest settlers traded with the Native American people. We call it bartering. The colonists gave the Native Americans things they thought they wanted or needed in exchange for the land. Perhaps you noticed English pounds and shillings. Pounds and shillings were English money used not only in the country of England but also in the English colonies in America.

You may be curious as to the value of two English pounds in wampum. Our first story told us that wampum was white or purple beads made from clam or quahog shells.

The early settlers in Plymouth established a court. The court in Plymouth was the only court for a long time. It met four times a year. In 1640, the Plymouth court set a rate of exchange for wampum. They did this in an effort to be fair to the First Americans. (Remember, making wampum was very slow, tiring work.) The court decided that six pieces of wampum would have the same value as one Spanish penny, which is two American cents. The members of the court felt that one Spanish dollar was worth about three hundred pieces of wampum. The court also decided that it would take 1,500 pieces of wampum to have the value of one pound (English money used by the colonists).

DISAPPEARANCE OF MANY NATIVE AMERICANS

When Dartmouth was purchased in 1652, Massasoit promised to remove, within a year, all the Native American people who lived there.

That proved the hardest part of the arrangement to put into operation. Indeed, it would have been impossible to do. Naturally, the Native Americans did not want to leave their homes. However, there were not nearly as many Native Americans living in Dartmouth in 1652 as there were when Gosnold explored the shores in 1602.

Perhaps you were wondering what happened to all the Native Americans. About 1618, a very serious epidemic caused many, many Native Americans to die. The Native Americans referred to this as "the time of great sorrow." The native population fell from about 30,000 to approximately 4,000.

THE DEED

When someone buys a piece of land, he gets a deed for the land. A deed is really a piece of paper that tells where the boundaries of the land are and who bought it. The white settlers had a deed of our town. Not all, but some of the purchasers' names were on the deed. One part of the deed says: "Massasoit and Wamsutta (Massasoit's older son) sold to William Bradford, Captain Myles Standish, Thomas Southworth, John Winslow, John Cooke, and their associates ..."

Whose name headed the list of purchasers? Yes, William Bradford headed the list. He was the governor of Plymouth Colony. Governor Bradford kept a record of early Plymouth Colony. When you study American history, you will learn more about Governor Bradford.

The name of Captain Myles Standish is next on the list. He was in charge of the Plymouth militia (guards or army). One of America's greatest and best beloved poets, Henry Wadsworth Longfellow, wrote a famous poem about Myles Standish. It is called, "The Courtship of Miles Standish." You will probably read it when you are in a higher grade in school.

John Cooke was another purchaser. He was one of the few purchasers who actually came to live in Dartmouth. John Cooke had come to America as a passenger on the Mayflower in 1620. That meant he was one of the Pilgrims. He was only a boy at that time. When he grew up, he became a Baptist minister. He was forced to leave Plymouth because his religious views differed from those of the Plymouth Colony. He settled in the Fairhaven section of Old Dartmouth. There is a monument to John Cooke in Fairhaven. Cooke was the last survivor of the Pilgrims who landed in Plymouth in 1620.

Not all the purchasers signed the paper that recorded the sale of Dartmouth. John Cooke and John Winslow signed for the colonists. Massasoit's older son, Wamsutta, signed for the Native Americans. Since Massasoit could not write, he left his mark. His mark looked like this: M M .

DARTMOUTH'S NAME

Although the sale took place on November 29, 1652, the deed was not recorded until June, 1664. How many years later was that? This time the paper was signed by Massasoit's younger son, Philip.

Our town received its name then, too. The original charter says, "The said town bee henceforth called and knowne by the name Dartmouth."

How did the settlers select the name Dartmouth? We feel that Dartmouth, Massachusetts, was named for Dartmouth, England. Why do we feel that way? The Pilgrims who came to Plymouth set sail from Plymouth, England. Originally, the Pilgrims set sail in two ships, the Mayflower and the Speedwell. Only the Mayflower reached America. What happened to the Speedwell? The two ships started out together from Plymouth,

England, but soon ran into trouble. They had to sail back into the harbor at Dartmouth, England for repairs. The Speedwell needed so many repairs that she was left behind. Her passengers were transferred to the Mayflower and she continued on the voyage. Remember, the early purchasers of Dartmouth, Massachusetts were from Plymouth, Massachusetts. Perhaps these settlers wished to use the names of the two English towns from which they had embarked. Thus, we have the names Plymouth and Dartmouth as towns in Massachusetts.

There is another explanation of how Dartmouth might have been chosen as the name of our town. Gosnold's ship, the Concord, hailed from Dartmouth. England. When the Concord returned to England, Gosnold and his crew spoke very favorably about our locality. Probably some of the people in Dartmouth, England, decided they would like to come here to live. Maybe they wanted to name this new town after their native town in England. Dartmouth, England is on a river mouth just the same as is Dartmouth, Massachusetts. This might have further influenced the early settlers to name our locality, Dartmouth.

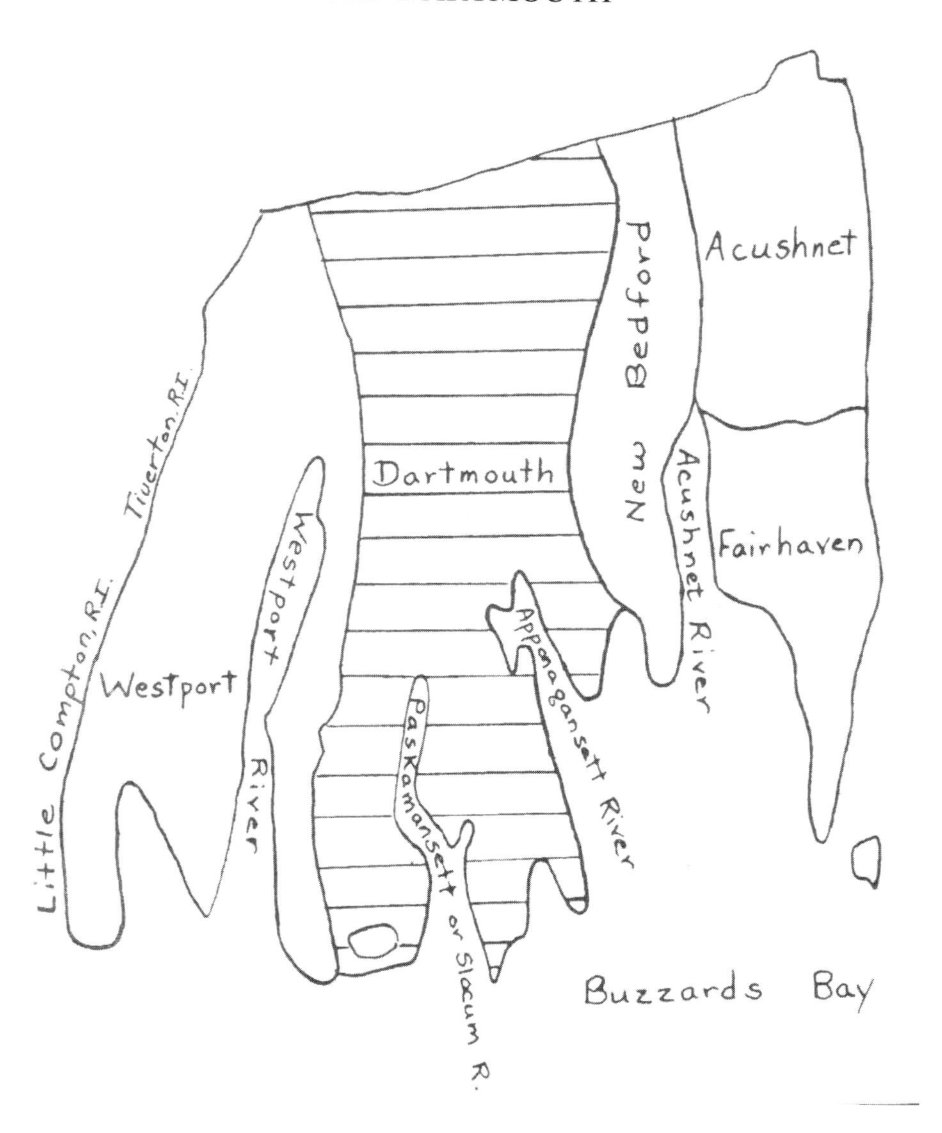

The Town of Dartmouth as it was originally in 1652. Very small sections of Little Compton, R.I. and Tiverton, R..I. also belonged to Dartmouth. The striped area shows Dartmouth as it has been since 1787.

DARTMOUTH'S SIZE

Was the Dartmouth of 1664 the same size as present-day Dartmouth? No, Dartmouth covered a greater area in 1664. In 1664, Dartmouth contained about 104 square miles. Now Dartmouth contains 61.4 square miles. About how much smaller is Dartmouth now? However, Dartmouth is still a large town in land area. In fact, we are the fourth largest town in the state of Massachusetts. But just imagine how large a town we would be if Dartmouth still extended over its original land!

When Dartmouth first became a town, it included present-day Dartmouth, New Bedford, Fairhaven, Acushnet, and Westport.

These places had Native American names. The Native Americans called New Bedford and Acushnet, Cushena. Cushena means "as far as the river." Dartmouth was known as Ponaganset. Sconticut was Fairhaven's name. Westport was known as Coakset. A small part of the towns of Tiverton, Rhode Island and Little Compton, Rhode Island were included in the original Dartmouth grant.

You might like to read a portion of the details of this real estate deal between Massasoit and the white settlers.

It is quite interesting. It said in part, "... all that tract or tracts of land lying three miles eastward from a river called Cushnet (Acushnet River) to a flat rock on the westward side of said harbor and with all the rivers, creeks, meadows, necks, and islands that lie in and before the same, and from the sea upward to go so high that the English may not be annoyed by the hunting of the Native Americans in any sort of their cattle."

The boundaries of our town were not very exact at the time of the purchase. The people who bought the land could be sure of only one of the boundaries. That was the thirteen miles of shoreline bordering Buzzards Bay.

Can you picture how our town looked 300 years ago?

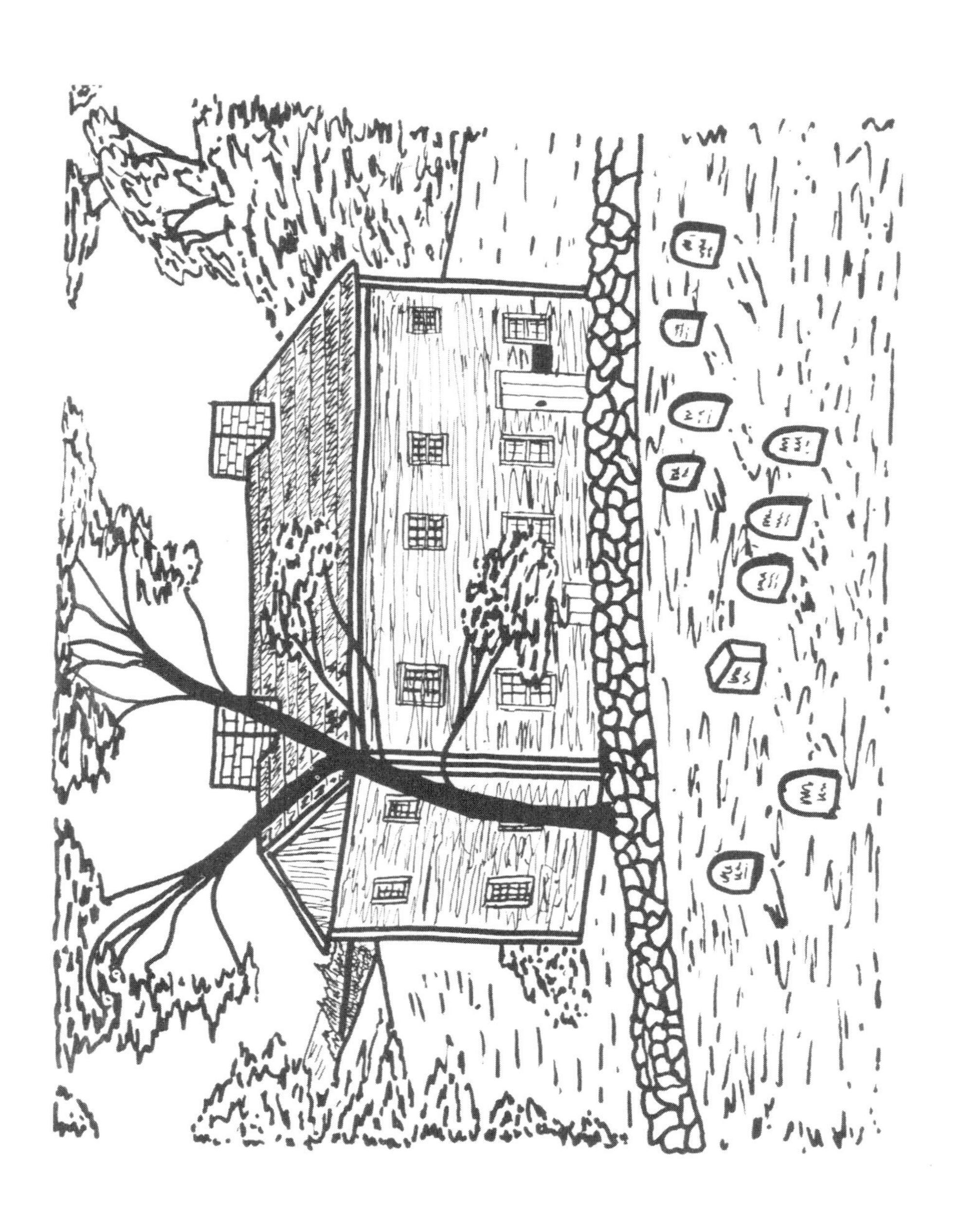

Apponegansett Meeting House

CHAPTER 4

DARTMOUTH'S EARLIEST SETTLERS

Have you always lived in Dartmouth or did you move here recently? If you moved here recently, do you know why your parents moved here? Would you like to know why the early settlers came to Dartmouth? Read this story and find out.

Why did Dartmouth's earliest white settlers come here? We know they did not come here because Dartmouth's soil was especially rich. They did not come here to take advantage of the fishing opportunities. Instead, they came here to enjoy religious freedom in their own way. This was especially true of the Baptists and the Quakers. They felt if they lived away from the large centers of population they could practice their religion in the manner they felt was right. These early Dartmouth settlers wished to be far away from the watchful eyes of the religious leaders in the other more prominent settlements in Massachusetts.

FIRST TEN FAMILIES

Many of Dartmouth's original settlers came here from the Plymouth Colony. You might say that Dartmouth was just beyond the border of the Plymouth Colony. Dartmouth was purchased by thirty-four people in the Plymouth Colony. Most of these purchasers never actually came here to reside. In reality, only ten of these purchasers (or the purchaser's family) came to live here. These ten families were:

Cook	Jenny
Delano	Kempton
Francis	Morton
Hicks	Samson
Howland	Soule

QUAKERS

Other early settlers in Dartmouth came from around Boston where the Puritans had formed Massachusetts Bay Colony. These were Quakers or "Friends" as we also called them. The Puritans wanted everyone to believe and worship in their way. They forced their form of religion on everyone who settled in the areas they claimed. (so did the Pilgrims.) Everyone had to pay taxes to support the Puritan Church, even if he was not a member of the Puritan Church.

The Quakers felt that was unfair. Because the Quakers did not practice their religion in the same way the Puritans did, the Quakers were not made welcome. Instead, they were fined and punished in all sorts of ways for disobeying Puritan laws. Many unpleasant things happened to them. Very frequently, they were forced to leave the Puritan settlements. Thus, in most cases the Quakers had no other choice but to seek happiness elsewhere. One of the places to which they went was Dartmouth. Here they hoped they would be far enough away from the Puritan Church to worship as they wished without being persecuted.

Quakers began to move here around the year 1657. The Tuckers, Babcocks, Allens, Giffords, Kirbys, and Wings moved into Dartmouth then from Cape Cod as well as the Boston area.

RHODE ISLANDERS

About the same time, still another group of people moved into Dartmouth, but they came for a different reason. They did not come here because of religious persecution. Rather, they moved here because there was not enough land for all of them where they were. These new land seekers moved here from Portsmouth, Rhode Island, where the amount of land they could own was not large enough to please some settlers.

Some of these settlers moved to Dartmouth where they could purchase as much land as they needed. Rhode Islanders moving here bore the following names:

Akin	Davis
Almy	Devoll
Anthony	Earle
Cadman	Lake
Chase	Mosher
Cornell	Ricketson

These original settlers came first to Russells Mills, Slocum Neck, and Smith's Neck. (The Native American name for Smith's Neck was Nomquid.) Soon, these settlers moved into Smith Mills, and lastly into what is now Fairhaven and New Bedford.

HARD WORK

These early settlers worked hard, but they were used to hard work. Although some of the woods had already been cleared by the Native Americans, there was still much more land to be cleared. These early pioneers in Dartmouth had a hard task for they only had a few tools and their own strong hands to do the work. An axe and a saw were tools necessary for trees to be cut down, not only to clear the land for farming, but also to use in building their houses. Wood was used for fuel, too.

Their tools were the simplest. In the beginning, most of them had hoes but no plows. With the aid of a hoe, they planted corn, wheat, oats, peas, and beans. The hoe also helped them keep the weeds from the hills of their growing crops. Later they would cut the grain crops with a sickle or a scythe. They also planted fruit trees such as apple and pear trees; for they found that most fruits that could be grown in England could also be grown here.

Do you recall that Gosnold spoke of our "fair meadows?" Hay grows in the meadows, doesn't it? Our early settlers found a plentiful supply of this wild grass. After it was cut and dried, they used it as feed for the cattle and sheep they had brought with them. They also brought pigs. In the fall, some of the cattle and hogs were killed for food. Do you know how they prepared the meat so it would not spoil? Did you guess that they smoked or salted it?

RALPH AND JOHN RUSSELL

One of Dartmouth's historians, Daniel Ricketson, tells us that Ralph Russell was one of Dartmouth's earliest residents, moving here in the mid 1600s. Mr. Ricketson claims that Ralph Russell moved to our town from Taunton. Mr. Ricketson further claims that Ralph Russell established the first iron forge in our town. It was supposed to have been in Russells Mills. We cannot be sure that Mr. Russell established an iron forge here. However, we are sure that his son, John Russell, became Dartmouth's first representative at the General Court in Plymouth. That was in the year 1665.

What is the longest walk you have ever taken? Were you tired? It was about 40 miles to Plymouth from Dartmouth. Mr. Russell walked both ways when he attended sessions of the General Court in Plymouth. That seems like a very long walk, but we should remember that people walked more in those days than we do now. Mr. Russell followed old Native American trails that led through the forest.

Apparently, Mr. John Russell had a fairly large house. Up until the late 1600s, the town meetings were held at his house. After Mr. Russell died, the voters gathered at the "home of widow Russell."

Do you recall that Captain Myles Standish was one of the original purchasers of Dartmouth? He paid only five or ten dollars for his share. Nine years later, on March 20, 1661, the John Russell you read about in the previous paragraph bought Myles Standish's share of Dartmouth. Mr. Russell paid Myles Standish $210.00 for the land. Mr. Russell's land was in what we now call Padanaram. It contained 3,200 acres. The land ran to Bush Street (the old Padanaram School, now used by the School

Department, is on Bush Street) north to Russells Mills Road (the Town Hall is located on Russells Mills Road). John Russell's share also included Bliss Corner and the land adjacent to Clark's Cove (New Bedford).

John Russell, his wife Dorothy, and their three sons built a large home on the east shore of the Apponegansett River in Padanaram. Russell was a successful farmer. Early historians say he had splendid apple orchards.

MILITIA AND LAW

Because of the constant threat of Native American uprisings, early towns were required to have a militia. In 1667, two men, Sergeant James Shaw and Arthur Hathaway, were appointed to organize a militia in Dartmouth. It was their task to drill the men in the use of arms. In 1671, the population of the town had increased so much, two more appointments were made to the militia. John Smith was made a lieutenant. (Some people believe this same Lt. John Smith is buried in a peaceful shaded cemetery off the road on Little River Road, South Dartmouth.) Jacob Mitchell was appointed ensign bearer. What is an ensign? What would be the duty of the ensign bearer? It was a wise move on the part of the early residents to have all the men trained in the use of arms. In another story, you will find out how that training helped them.

At a town meeting, the rules or laws for running the town are discussed and decided upon. A Dartmouth town meeting was called for July 22, 1674. In those days, only men had the right to vote. At this July meeting, it was voted that "All the town meetings do begin at ten of the clock and to continue until the moderator (the person in charge of the meeting) duly relieved the town, not exceeding four of the clock." Do we have a special hour when our meetings start now? Can you find out who the present moderator is?

"That all such people as to neglect to appear at the town meeting, shall forfeit to the town one shilling and six pence a piece, and for coming to the meeting too late, three pence an hour." Are people fined today if they fail to attend a meeting or if they come in late?

In the next year, 1675, there was a complaint about the condition of some of the fences. A gentlemen was given authority to "view men's fences and to notify them for a sufficient fence or condemn them and give men warnings when they has to mend them." In the days when each settler owned many sheep and other animals, it was the duty of the fence viewer to make sure each farmer keep his share of the fence in good repair to prevent the animals from wandering into the field and eating the crops. Many of these so-called fences were actually rambling stone walls.

Thus, we can see that our infant town was beginning to progress.

CHAPTER 5

KING PHILIP'S WAR
1675–1678

Did you ever become angry with a friend of yours? Did you disagree because you felt he had taken something that belonged to you?

This story is about a Native American chief who fought the white people because he thought they took something that belonged to the Native Americans.

The people of Dartmouth first learned about war in their own backyard.

MASSASOIT'S FRIENDSHIP

You have probably already learned that when the Pilgrims landed in Plymouth in 1620, one Native American sachem (chief) was very good to them. Massasoit was that sachem. Massasoit was very kind, friendly, and fair to the early white settlers. Because of his attitude, it was possible for the white people to live in harmony and friendship with the Native Americans. As long as he lived, there was peace between the white men and the First Americans. Massasoit lived about forty years after signing a friendly pact, called *The Treaty of Peace,* with the Pilgrims in Plymouth. For forty years then, there were friendly relations between the Native Americans and the colonists. Massasoit deserves most of the credit for that because he never went back on the promises he made in *The Treaty of Peace.*

WAMSUTTA

The Native Americans were usually known by two names; one was their Native American name and the other, the name given to them by the English. When Massasoit died, he was succeeded by his elder son, Wamsutta, or Alexander. Wamsutta was his Native American name. The white people usually called him Alexander. Alexander did not rule long. Some white people thought Wamsutta was plotting with other Native Americans to harm the settlers. He was asked to go to Plymouth to explain his actions and to show evidence of the same loyalty his father had. Wamsutta went to Plymouth. The leaders of Plymouth found Wamsutta not guilty of trying to harm the white settlers. Unfortunately, on his way back home from Plymouth, Wamsutta became ill and died.

Wamsutta's younger brother, Philip, blamed the white settlers for Wamsutta's death. Philip believed the white people had poisoned Wamsutta.

PHILIP BECOMES SACHEM

When Wamsutta died, Philip, who was twenty-four years of age, became sachem (chief) of the Native Americans in this area. The colonists called him King Philip. His Native American name was Metacom. He was proud, clever, and an excellent speaker. Generally speaking, he did not like the white settlers. Knowing this, the white settlers forced him and his followers to give up the seventy guns they had brought to a treaty meeting held in 1672 in Taunton. Philip disagreed with his father's policy of friendliness and trust. As was mentioned before, he blamed the white people for the death of his brother Wamsutta.

By this time, most of the Native Americans were using guns instead of bows and arrows. Where did the Native Americans get so many guns? The Native Americans secured guns, gunpowder, and knives from the white settlers. When the white people wanted corn or land, some Native Americans would not accept anything in trade except the white men's weapons. Other whites did not hesitate to sell guns and ammunition to the Native Americans. Philip knew where he could buy firearms. He bought some from the French Canadians. Research tells us that before the war ended, Philip had to go as far as New York to get some ammunition.

In fairness to the Native Americans, we should try to understand why Philip might have hated the English settlers. Philip knew how good his father, Massasoit, had been to the white men. Many settlers bought their land from the Native

Americans. They paid for it in guns, blankets, knives, and jewelry. But not all settlers were fair to the Native Americans. Some took the land without paying for it. Others did not trade fairly with the Native Americans. Sometimes when trading furs and skins with the Native Americans, the settlers gave them valueless trinkets.

Then, too, Philip could see more and more white-faced people moving into what was once the Native American's own territory. The Native Americans felt the hunting grounds and all the land belonged to all of them. They did not understand the white man's idea of private ownership of land. They did not understand why the colonists pushed them out of their land. The Native Americans dreaded the white-faced strangers. They thought the white man would be their master and would make slaves out of them. Some early English sea captains had seized some Native Americans, taken them out of this country, and sold them as slaves. All these things made Philip angry with the white men. He realized his people were getting poorer. Since he was proud, it hurt him to see his people being driven away from their land. This we can understand.

Philip said to a friend, "They (the white people) disarmed my people. But a small part of the dominion of my ancestors remains. I am determined not to live until I have no country."

TROUBLE BEGINS

Actually, a short time after settlers began to move into Dartmouth, Philip started to do small things to annoy them. But it was not until after Massasoit died that Philip really began to trouble the settlers.

One day Philip sent gifts to other Native American sachems scattered throughout what is now eastern Massachusetts and Rhode Island. He asked the other Native American sachems to help him drive out all the white men. Not all Native American tribes were friendly to the white people. Some Native American sachems did help Philip. Throughout Massachusetts, the Native Americans made sudden attacks on the settlers. They practically wiped out settlement after settlement by these surprise attacks.

PROTECTION FROM THE NATIVE AMERICANS

How could settlers protect themselves from the Native Americans? For protection, the settlers built blockhouses or stockades. In some towns, settlers' houses were turned into blockhouses. These strong houses were built to resist the Native American attacks.

In our town, the settlers had two places to go when seeking safety. One was in Padanaram. It was on the east bank of the Apponegansett River at the foot of Wilson Street, not too far from where Elm Street and Russells Mills Road meet. There, a stockade had been built around the home of John Russell. When King Philip's War broke out in 1675, John Russell fortified his home with a garrison and stockade.

What does the dictionary say about a stockade? Does it say that a stockade had strong high walls built of close-fitting logs standing upright in the ground? Does it tell you there were holes or slits in the walls to shoot through? Does it tell you a stockade had a high strong, gate that could be barred up tight when necessary? A stockade has all these things. This Dartmouth stockade was sometimes called, "Russell's Garrison" or "Garrison at Russell's Orchard in Ponagansett." (Russell's home was referred to as "The Castle.")

Russell's Garrison was about twenty feet square. Maybe some day your teacher will help you measure off a twenty foot square on the playground so you can see just how big Russell's Garrison was. On the south side of the garrison, a ten-foot square had been added. There was a brook close by where people could get necessary water. A Native American settlement and fort was on the opposite side of the Apponegansett River. The Native Americans who lived there were friendly.

The other place where the Dartmouth settlers could feel safe was in present-day Fairhaven. It was the home of John Cooke. Remember, John Cooke was one of the original purchasers of Dartmouth. A stockade was built around his home, too. John Cooke's stockade was at the end of the Coggeshall Street Bridge in Fairhaven. Do you know where that is?

METHOD OF ATTACK

The Native Americans liked to attack suddenly. There were not very many Native Americans and they thought if they attacked suddenly and quickly, they probably would not lose many men. They were right, of course. In the beginning, the Native Americans probably hoped they could scare all the white people away. But they could not scare the new settlers away. The white people had no intention of leaving here. The white men had turned their backs on their old homes in Europe and intended to permanently remain in America.

King Philip's War spread quickly. Everywhere, people felt in danger of the Native Americans. In several villages, the homes were burned and people killed. Some white people were carried off as captives.

THE DARTMOUTH TREATY

In Dartmouth, a treaty had been made between the local Native Americans and the settlers. The Native Americans promised they would not attack the settlers. The settlers promised that no harm would come to the local Native Americans.

Captain Samuel Eels was in charge of Russell's Garrison in Dartmouth. On July 21, 1676, Captain Benjamin Church and his army arrived at Russell's Garrison. Captain Church had been sent by the officials of Plymouth Colony. Captain Church was a good soldier. He and his small army spent the night at Russell's Garrison. They did not build a fire, as it would have attracted the enemy across the river.

The next day, Captain Church saw a band of Native Americans. He chased them in the direction of Smith Mills. There he captured many of them.

Remember, the settlers in Dartmouth had promised no harm would come to the local Native Americans. Unfortunately, that promise was not kept. Many Dartmouth Native Americans went to the garrison for protection and security. However, later, these Dartmouth Native Americans were among the 160 Native

Americans that Captain Church marched to Plymouth. In fairness to Captain Church, it should be noted that he wanted to honor the Dartmouth treaty, but higher officials in Plymouth overruled him. Church's son later wrote, "This action was so hateful to Captain Church that he opposed it to the loss of the good will and respect of some that before were his good friends."

Eighty of these Native Americans taken to Plymouth by Captain Church were Dartmouth Native Americans. They were marched from Russell's Garrison to Clark's Cove. They followed an old Native American path. They then walked through the forest of present-day New Bedford and Acushnet to Plymouth, again following Native American trails. In Plymouth, the Native Americans were sold as slaves. As slaves, the Native American captives were shipped out of this country and taken to the West Indies. Can you locate the West Indies on the map? Among the Native Americans that were sold as slaves were King Philip's wife, Wootonakansuta, and his nine-year-old son. A letter from Mr. Cotton to Dr. Mather in March 1667 contains the remark, "Philips's boy goes to be sold."

ATTACK ON DARTMOUTH

Now the Native Americans really were angry. Philip had been waiting for a chance to strike a blow. The sale of his wife and son was more than he could bear, for the Native Americans loved their families dearly. The Native Americans attacked. Dartmouth was one of the areas attacked fiercely.

"To the garrison! The Indians are on the warpath!" was the cry heard. Many settlers heard the warning in time. They fled from their cabins and found safety at either Russell's Garrison or Cooke's Garrison. Those who fled were the only Dartmouth settlers who escaped to tell the story. Others were not so fortunate. Settlers in Dartmouth were widely scattered. Not all of them heard the warning. They were caught unaware by the Native Americans.

There were about thirty-seven homes in Dartmouth at that time. All of these were burned. The Native Americans burned the barns and sheds, too. They destroyed all the crops belonging to the settlers. Cattle, too, were slain. The people who had not found shelter were cruelly killed. Dartmouth was left in ruins.

CAPTAIN CHURCH'S VICTORY

Most of the white people did not know the Native American way of fighting. Using arrows, they usually shot from the protection of the trees. The Native Americans would strike and move quickly from place to place. They often hid in dark swamps.

But one white man did know the Native American way of fighting. That man was Captain Benjamin Church. Captain Church was still trying to catch Philip. He scoured the woods looking for him. Captain Church knew the ways of the Native Americans. He knew better how to fight them than did most of the white people. He also knew how to make friends with the Native Americans. When Captain Church was hunting for Philip, he had more Native Americans than white soldiers helping him. He and his man hunted from place to place without catching Philip. At one time, Captain Church again returned to Dartmouth. This time he captured some unfriendly Native Americans.

Finally, a friendly Native American told Captain Church that Philip and his followers were hiding in a swamp where they thought they would be safe. Philip and his men were running short of food. Church and his men flushed out Philip and his followers. In trying to run away, Philip was caught and killed by a Native American helping Captain Church. This cruel war ended with Philip's death.

The time of King Philip's War was referred to as, "... black and fatal days, the saddest that ever befell New England," King Philip's War certainly caused much sadness in our town.

Captain Church hunting for King Philip.

You might be interested in seeing the partially restored Russell Garrison sometime. It is on Fort Street at the end of Lucy Street in Padanaram. Owned by the Old Dartmouth Historical Society, the site has a fieldstone monument which reads:

"THE RUSSELL GARRISON
A place of refuge for the
early settlers of Dartmouth during
KING PHILIP'S WAR 1675–1676
Foundations restored by the
Old Dartmouth Historical Society 1951"

CHAPTER 6

DARTMOUTH GROWS LARGER

"My, how you have grown!" How many times has someone said that to you or your brothers and sisters? Most likely, you have heard that remark many times.

You can tell when you have grown taller and put on weight. The clothes you wore last year are now too small or too short for you. Of course, gaining weight and growing taller are not the only ways you grow. Each year you grow in many different ways. When you do, some changes have to be made.

Towns grow, too. This story will tell you some changes that were made as our town of Dartmouth grew from a settlement of less than a dozen families to a town of more than one thousand people.

Because the town of Dartmouth had suffered so great a loss of homes, animals, and crops during the King Philip's War, the people of Dartmouth did not have to pay taxes to Plymouth Colony for a few years. This was a big help because most of the town's inhabitants had lost practically everything they owned.

Although the Plymouth Court offered help in the form of exemption from paying taxes for a few years, it scolded the settlers, too. The Court pointed out that the Native American trouble was probably God's way of punishing the people of Dartmouth for not worshipping God the same way they did. This proves that the Pilgrims were out of sympathy with those who did not worship God in the exact way they did.

The Court also ordered the Dartmouth settlers to build their homes close together for safety's sake. But the settlers could not do this even if they wanted to do so. Dartmouth settlers were, for the most part, farmers. Therefore, they had to build where the land was suitable for farming.

But the assistance given by the Plymouth Court was not the only help the Dartmouthites received. Help, in the from of money, came to them from thousands of miles away. Early town records reveal that Great Britain and especially Ireland, generously sent money to aid the sufferers of King Philip's War.

Dartmouth was given the second highest amount of money from the gift sent to America by the Irish and the Britains.

In a few short years after King Phillip's War, the townspeople regained their courage. How hard they worked to reestablish their town! They began to face the reality that to survive they needed to rebuild their town and clear more land. While clearing the land for farming, the settlers also began to build the stone walls we now see in many places in Dartmouth. How the early settlers must have labored to pile up such heaps of rocks into long stone walls!

By June 20, 1678, the town had recovered enough to have its first town meeting since King Philip's War. Town officials were again selected. Women were not allowed to vote. Not all men could vote. A man could only vote if he owned land.

STRANGE LAWS

Sometimes in these early town meetings, the townspeople made laws which seem strange to us. You might be interested in some of these laws concerning animals. The woods of Dartmouth abounded in wild animals. These animals were one danger with which the early settlers had to cope. Apparently, the Native Americans helped greatly in killing off those wild animals. At a town meeting held May 29, 1685, it was voted, "... that where it doth appear that Indian Robbins living in Sogonset did kill a wolf sometime this year within the Township, that he shall have six shillings and that any Indian or Indians that shall kill any wolves hereafter shall have six shillings paid unto him for such wolves or bears so killed."

In the year 1684, it was ordered that the Indians be allowed to hunt, provided, "... that they do kill three wolves, or three bears or pay ten shillings (English money) to each village." It also "... ordered that the English shall have teen (ten) shillings for the killing of a wolf or bear." This law points out that there must have been many wolves and bears in Dartmouth three hundred years ago. Are there any wolves here now?

It may interest you to learn that the wolves were also very troublesome to the Pilgrims in Plymouth. The Pilgrims were forced to have an armed guard watch their fields for a few weeks after planting seeds. Otherwise, the hungry wolves would dig up the fish planted to fertilize the seeds. It would seem as if the early Dartmouth settlers had the same problem since they were obliged to go about armed at all times as a protection against wild animals.

In 1686, the townspeople voted to have a pound made. What is a pound used for? Do we have a town pound now? In 1707, a town pound was again mentioned. This time the townspeople voted that the pound must have a "Convenient" gate with iron hinges and a lock.

The original pound, located at the Russells Mills section of Dartmouth, is still standing. This pound is in good condition. Try to see it sometime. It is on Russells Mills Road close to the Russells Mills library. If you travel from Padanaram to Russells Mills, the pound will be on your left. It is close to the road.

The pound is made of stone except for the gate. Notice that there is a ledge in back of it. How might that help? Any stray animal kept in this pound until his master called for him was fed by the man who lived in the house adjacent to the pound. Of course, when the owner came to claim his animal, he had to pay a fine for letting his animal stray. He also had to pay for the food the animal ate.

Do you ever think of birds as being a nuisance? In the year 1704, the town required "... that every householder being a planter shall kill twelve blackbirds between the first day of January and the middle of May yearly, on pain of forfeiting (giving up) three half pence for every bird they shall neglect killing of said number." They also ordered, "... that for every blackbird that shall be killed within the time limit over the number or twelve, each planter shall be paid one penny out of the town stock."

They made this law because the crows and blackbirds ate the corn and the fruits. Do we need this law now? In addition, the town voted that each crow killed would count as three blackbirds. Which bird did the settlers feel was the bigger pest? What makes you think so?

In the year 1713, much of Dartmouth was still forested. The wolves were continuing to cause trouble and alarm. Therefore, the townspeople voted, "… that twenty shillings shall be given to each person that shall kill a wolf within the township of Dartmouth." What does that mean? Don't you imagine that in the wintertime the men and the older boys who liked adventure often went hunting to get rid of some of these wolves and other wild animals? Naturally, they would be interested in earning the twenty-shilling reward, too.

Another animal is mentioned in the records of 1721. The town records of that year said the voters agreed, "… that all geese running at large from the first day of April to the last day of October without their wings cut and without a yoke upon them shall be placed in the town pound, and the owner of such geese shall pay one penny apiece for pounding the same." Why did they want the wings of the geese cut?

The law further stated that there had to be a "… sufficient fence around any pond, river, or cove where any geese were swimming over any of the waters into any field, meadow, or pasture it shall be lawful for the owner of such land forthwith to take up all such geese and pound them in any yard or house as they may have."

Besides paying one-penny apiece to get back his geese, the owner also had to pay for any damage the geese might have done.

If the geese got out again, the owner would have to pay a larger sum of money to get them back. You may wonder why settlers kept geese. Geese are delicious food. Geese also make good watchdogs. They make loud noises which serve as a warning. They'll fight, too. Their feathers were used for pillows and mattresses. The quills make fine pens for writing. (Remember, there were no ball point pens then.)

Still another animal was referred to in the town meeting of 1722. The inhabitants voted that there shall be "… three shillings allowed for any grown wildcat that shall be killed within our township from the last day of September to the first day of

March yearly to the person or persons that kill them." They also added, "... and six shillings for each wildcat killed the other part of the year." During what months of the year did they pay the most for wildcats? Aren't you glad that these wildcats, which were once so numerous, have disappeared?

What is meant by domesticated animals? Domesticated animals are also mentioned in the town records. The settlers were required to have a mark notched in the ear of each cattle. You might call this a form of branding the cattle. The ear mark had to be registered with the town clerk. This was necessary since the cattle were allowed to roam loose in the fields. Hogs, too, were allowed to roam around. The town record of March 1728, reads as follows: "Voted that hogs may go at large."

What do the early Dartmouth records say about these birds and animals?

ENGLISH-STYLE PUNISHMENTS

Many of our early colonists came from England. By now you have learned that England had strict laws for wrongdoings. People who broke the laws were punished in ways which seem strange today. Some of the punishments were very severe. Naturally, the early colonists brought many of these forms of punishment with them. One means of punishment was called the stocks. Stocks consisted of a wooden frame with two large boards. The holes were cut out in the center of the boards where the two boards came together. For punishment, a person might have to sit with his feet, or feet and hands, caught in the stocks. The large boards were separated until the man's feet were set in place. Then the boards were placed together and locked. Of course, the man could not get his feet out then. How painful it was to sit that way for any length of time! He was further shamed by wearing a card around his neck telling his wrongdoing. Often people would stand and stare at the one being punished. The onlookers sometimes ridiculed the man in the stocks. It was considered all right for them to do so. Occasionally someone threw things at him.

The early Dartmouth residents used some of these English ways of punishing people. How do we know this? We know this is true because in 1686 it was voted that John Russell should make a pair of stocks for Dartmouth.

Another method of punishment that originated in England was the whipping post. Almost all the early towns in America had a whipping post. The whipping post was a tall stout post to which a standing man could be tied. The man was stripped to his waist. While tied, the man was given blows on his bare back. A leather whip was used. Part of the man's punishment included having other people watch him get punished. We would not like this kind of punishment.

But like every other community in those days, Dartmouth had a whipping post. In 1709, the townspeople voted to have Henry Howland "… make a pair of stocks and a whipping post." Whipping posts were used in Dartmouth as late as 1785. Mr. George Taber said his mother was present at the last public whipping which was given in the Fairhaven section of Old Dartmouth. For such an event, bells were rung as a signal that someone was to be punished. School was dismissed so the pupils could witness the punishment. Spectators were welcome because it was felt they would make the wrongdoer feel more ashamed. Around 1800 this type of punishment was stopped. That must have made the people happy because most people did not enjoy seeing other people punished.

OTHER LAWS

Let us look at a few other laws the early Dartmouthites thought necessary.

By 1686, the town had grown large enough to require a meetinghouse. (How many years had passed since the town had been organized?) That year the voters ordered that a meetinghouse be built "… 24 feet long, 16 feet wide, 9 feet stud (what does that mean?) and to be covered with long shingles, and to be enclosed with planks and clapboards, and to have an under floor laid, and to be benched around, and to have a table to it suitable to the length of said house. Also for two light windows." Did you notice how many important details were included?

Apparently, the building was not erected immediately for as late as 1694 the town records prove the meetings were held at the home of John Russell. But the building was built soon after that.

By 1739, the townspeople desired a new town house with "… convenient glass windows and shutters." Three men were selected to supervise the building of this new town house. They were also to see that the old town house was sold or pulled down. Where are our town meetings held now?

The early townspeople looked with disfavor on people who did not work. To them, laziness was sinful. In 1742, a workhouse was open for "… the setting to work of all idle persons." Eighteen years later, in 1760, James Smith was given permission to live in the workhouse for two years at $5.00 a year. Mr. Smith was to use the $5.00 to make repairs on the workhouse. The voters gave him the right to "… take care of all the poor and idle persons that shall be sent to him to keep them in labor (work)." A workhouse is again mentioned in the town records of 1773 when the townspeople voted to build a new workhouse in the Bedford section of Dartmouth.

As early as 1747 there was some thought on the part of the villagers in Acushnet of separating the present town of Acushnet from Dartmouth. But the town voted that Acushnet village should not be separated from Dartmouth. The people of Acushnet had to wait another forty years before their wish was fulfilled. What year would that be?

Have you ever heard of seining fish? When men fish with a seine, they use a large circular fish net. The seine is held upright in the water by weights or floats. When it is hauled in, it is pulled by its ends. Thus, the fish are caught in the middle.

On May 21, 1771, the townspeople voted "… to lay a duty of two Shilling Lawful Money per Barrel on all fish Seigned within the harbors or covers of this Town the present year." Can you think of any reason why this law might have been passed?

It may interest you to know that as early as the 1700s Dartmouth had fish inspectors. Do we have fish inspectors now? What do you think the duties of a fish inspector would be?

DARTMOUTH IN 1768

In 1768, nineteen years before New Bedford, Fairhaven, and Acushnet were separated from our town, we find these facts about Old Dartmouth. The population of the town was 5,033. In that year, there were 722 dwelling houses in our town. Also, there were 158 tanneries, slaughterhouses, and other workhouses.

In a slaughterhouse, animals are slaughtered (killed). Then the hides or skin of the animals are removed. Finally, the flesh of the animal is butchered to be sold as meat in the stores.

The hides of animals are treated and preserved in the form of leather in a tannery. The man who ran the tannery was called a tanner. He was kept busy, as people often wore leather garments such as caps, boots, breeches, and aprons. (Children wore leather aprons to school.) Leather was also used for saddles, buckles, and mugs.

Thirty gristmills, fulling mills, and sawmills were located here in 1768.

Wheat, corn, or barley are ground into flour at a gristmill. The first settlers in Dartmouth had to grind their grain using a wooden mortar and pestle. That was a very slow way to do it. They knew they had to have a way to grind corn more quickly. Therefore, gristmills were built along the streams. The water flowed over the wheel alongside the mill. The water forced the wheel to turn. This provided the power for the gristmill. Remember, the women of the families did all their own baking in those days. They used more flour than most of us today. The farmers loaded the corn or wheat they had raised into a wagon and transported it to the gristmill. The man who worked at the mill was called a miller. The farmers waited while the miller ground the grain into flour. Can you see why the miller was a big help in a town?

Woolen cloth was made thicker and fuller in a fulling mill. In the early days of our country, most of the settlers raised their own sheep. Sheep are very useful animals. They give us food. They also give us wool. Once a year the wool was sheared or cut from the sheep. When it was cut, it was soft and thick and long. Cloth was made from the wool. The cloth was usually woven in the home by the women. The spinning wheel and the handloom were important items in the early American homes. There were no stores where they could buy cloth; therefore, the ladies had to make the cloth. Sometimes flax was combined with the wool. Linen is made from flax. Since flax was grown in Dartmouth, no doubt it was sometimes used in combination with wool.

Sawmills were time savers for the pioneers. After the early farmers cut down trees, they hauled some of the logs to the sawmill. There the logs would be cut into finished lumber. The finished boards were used in building their homes and other buildings.

There was only one iron works in our town in 1768. Maybe that was because the iron found in the bogs around here was of a poor quality. At the iron works, chunks of iron were melted down. While hot, the iron could be pounded into different shapes. Tools, horseshoes, plows, shears, pots for cooking, wagon wheel rims, and iron works for ships were some of the things made at an iron works.

Much farming was carried on. Over 10,000 acres of land was used for pastures. A little more than two thousand acres of land was used for growing crops.

There were more animals than people in Dartmouth in 1768. The list of animals included: 797 oxen, 525 horses, 1,965 cows and heifers, 7,108 goats and sheep, and 383 hogs.

What animals were found in the largest number? Let's see if we can find out which animals are found in the largest number now. Why do you think the farmers kept so many oxen and horses? Why don't we have many of these animals now? What do goats give us? What is another name for hogs?

Do you think it fun to compare old-time Dartmouth with the Dartmouth you live in?

CHAPTER 7

MEN HAVE A TEA PARTY IN BOSTON

We usually think of tea parties as something just for ladies or little girls and their dolls. However, at this tea party, not one lady was present! What a strange tea party! Let's find out more about it.

Dartmouth played an important part in events leading up to the Revolutionary War. The following story will tell you about Dartmouth's role in this famous tea party.

THE UNFAIR TAXES

Massachusetts was one of the original thirteen English colonies. Because Massachusetts was an English colony, the English government thought it could make the settlers here pay taxes on certain goods. The English government put a tax on several things the English sold to the colonists.

The colonists did not like to pay taxes to the English. They said the king had no right to tax them if they couldn't help to make the laws. But the English king would not let the colonists help make the laws. The king did not think the colonists should have the same rights as the people in England. He said, "The colonies belong to England. They must do as we say. They must pay taxes to England!"

THE TAX ON TEA

Soon the English king learned that the colonists were very angry about the taxes. The king decided to remove all taxes on everything except tea. The colonists still objected. Again, they said, "If we cannot help make the laws, why should we pay a tax?"

The colonists said they would not pay the tea tax. The English king reminded them that the tax on tea was only a few cents on the pound. The colonists said, "We know it is only a few cents on each pound of tea. It isn't the amount of the tax; it is the

The Boston Tea Party

idea of being forced to pay a tax. Even if it was only a one cent tax on the pound of tea, we would be against it."

Now the English colonists liked tea very much. The English had been tea drinkers for a long time. But the unjust king told them they would have to buy the taxed tea or go without any tea. The colonists became very angry. They said, "We will go without tea rather than pay the tax on it. When the tea ships come into Boston Harbor, we will not let them remove the tea. We won't buy it. We won't even let it be brought into the country. It must not be unloaded. It will have to be sent back to England."

But the governor who had been sent to Boston by the English king said, "The tea must be landed. We will not send the tea back. These ships will not sail back to England until the tea has been landed."

The patriots had heard enough. They decided to take action. It took courage, but the patriots were very courageous. They held a protest meeting at the "Old South" meetinghouse in Boston. They voted to take action immediately. "We'll make Boston Harbor a teapot tonight!" the patriots said. That was December 16, 1773.

THE BOSTON TEA PARTY

Shortly after dark, a war whoop was heard in Boston. People living near the wharf where the tea ships were tied up, rushed to their windows and saw a number of Native Americans. But these Native Americans were not real Native Americans. They were white men dressed as Native Americans. They were clothed in blankets. They had painted their skin copper-colored. Do you wonder why the white men were disguised as Native Americans? They did this so the English governor and other officials could not recognize them. If they had been recognized, they might have been punished later by the English governor. The white men disguised as Native Americans had axes and hammers in their hands. They ran for the Boston wharf where the tea ships were. There was no uproar. Quickly and quietly they boarded the tea ships. Using their axes and hammers, they ripped open the tea cases and dumped the tea into the harbor. What pleasure it gave them to spill the tea into the sea! They made Boston Harbor a teapot.

A large crowd of people were on the wharf watching the "Native Americans." There was no disorder. The onlookers watched quietly, but happily. After throwing the three hundred and forty-two cases of tea over the sides of the ships, the "Native Americans" carefully swept up the decks of the ships where the tea cases had been opened. Not even a speck of tea remained. They put everything in order on the ships. They accidentally broke a padlock. They replaced it with a new one. They did not want to damage any property. The only wanted to unload the tea.

EXCITEMENT THROUGHOUT THE COLONIES

The news of the Boston Tea Party spread rapidly. Horseback riders carried the story throughout Massachusetts and to the other twelve colonies. As you can imagine, there was great excitement when the news reached the other colonists. People were delighted to hear what the Boston "Native Americans" had done. Bells were ringing and people shouting. In some country towns, bonfires were lit to celebrate this great event. It was a daring act to throw the tea overboard. After all, the colonies were small and England was very powerful at that time. England was then the most powerful country in the world. No wonder the colonists were overjoyed when they heard about the Boston Tea Party! They laughed about the large cup of tea they made for the fishes.

DARTMOUTH'S PART IN THE BOSTON TEA PARTY

Why has the story of the Boston Tea Party been included in this history of Dartmouth? Because "The Dartmouth" played a large part in this daring deed. A Dartmouth man, Henry Perkins, was a participant in the tea party. One of the tea ships was a Dartmouth ship. It was called "The Dartmouth." It had been built here by Dartmouth men. "The Dartmouth" was the first ship built in our town. It was launched in Dartmouth in 1767. It was owned by a Dartmouth man, Francis Rotch. Francis Rotch was a ship owner who made his living by carrying goods from one place to another.

Earlier in the year 1773, Mr. Rotch had sailed to England in "The Dartmouth" with a cargo of whale oil. This he sold in England. For the return trip back to America, the ship carried one hundred forty-four chests of tea. Boston merchants, loyal to the English government, paid for this tea, but we know they never received it because it was dumped into the harbor. Mr. Rotch was present at the protest meeting held in the "Old South" meetinghouse. He was scolded on all sides by the excited patriots. Mr. Rotch told the patriots he would like to sail out of the harbor without unloading his cargo of tea. But he also explained to the disturbed patriots that he could not get the permission of the English governor to do so because the governor was absent. Mr. Rotch tried several times to get this permission, but he was not successful.

Because of the Boston Tea Party, the people throughout the colonies said they would give up drinking tea. That was a big sacrifice because the colonists were really very fond of tea. People promised not to buy any more tea until the tax was removed.

Like all colonists, the residents of Dartmouth were against the tea tax. Also, like most Englishmen, they enjoyed a cup of tea. Tea was the favorite drink of the women in Dartmouth.

DARTMOUTH STANDS FIRM

In Dartmouth in January 1774, a meeting was called. That was a little more than a year after the Boston Tea Party. Both men and women went to the meeting, but there were more women than men. There were fifty-seven women who attended the meeting. The women agreed not to drink any more tea until the tax was removed. Instead, they promised to drink only homemade tea, probably made from the roots and flowers of the sassafras or perhaps from raspberry leaves. They probably felt they were fighting a battle for liberty by drinking the not-so-pleasing homemade tea. Learning that one local man had just purchased some tea, the women went to him and asked him to give it up. When this gentleman saw how serious the women were, he turned over to them the tea he had purchased.

Six months later, on July 18, 1774, a town meeting was held in Dartmouth. The tea tax was one of the things discussed. On that day the townspeople voted, "... that we will not purchase any goods manufactured in Great Britain and Ireland which shall be imported from thence after this day, that we will not purchase any goods from hawker, that we will not purchase any foreign tea whatever ..."

Thus, you see, the inhabitants of Dartmouth loyally joined with the rest of the colonists in refusing to support the tea tax.

CHAPTER 8

THE REVOLUTIONARY WAR
1775–1783

Do you know why we never have school on April 19th? April 19th, Patriot's Day, is a holiday. This story will tell you why April 19th is one of the important days in our history, for it marks the beginning of America's freedom and independence.

In the story of the Boston Tea Party, you learned that Massachusetts was one of the thirteen original colonies. We often say England was our mother country. In those days, it was thought that the colonies were for the benefit of the mother country.

As the mother country, England was forcing the colonists to pay taxes on certain items they bought. The colonists felt they should be allowed the same liberties as the Englishmen who lived in England. The colonists did not want to pay taxes to England. In fact, they refused to do so. These unfair taxes eventually resulted in war between England and the colonies. This was called the Revolutionary War. It was also referred to as the War of Independence because the thirteen colonies were fighting for their independence, or freedom. The war lasted about seven years. The American colonists won their independence in the Revolutionary War. Our thirteen separate little colonies eventually became our first thirteen states.

The Revolutionary War was very hard on the colonists. There were not many people in this country then. Most of the people were farmers. They did not have much money. The colonies only had a few trained soldiers. They had no navy. They were not really organized. Besides, they were fighting against England, the strongest and richest nation in the world at that time. The colonies probably would not have won the war without the aid of France, who sent men, money, and ships to help us. France's help came when we sadly needed it.

PREPARATION FOR WAR

You will learn more about this war when you study American history. For now, let's find out what part Dartmouth played in this war and in the years leading up to the war.

An excise tax is a tax on goods made in this country to be sold and used here. The colonists objected to this tax. In 1754, the Dartmouth residents said they would not pay the excise tax on wine and other liquors. People in other towns voted the same way. They also refused to pay the tax on the following fruits: limes, lemons, and oranges. These fruits were not grown here. We had to import them. They were brought here by English ships.

In 1756, the townspeople voted to purchase a supply of gunpowder and bullets to have on hand. Many of the townspeople did not believe in fighting, but made these purchases to be prepared should a need arise.

Eighteen years later, in 1774, the Dartmouthites stood firm with other towns and cities in the colonies. They voted not to obey some English laws. Some of them felt rather unhappy to go against English laws, but they realized it was necessary because the English laws were too harsh. There was one good reason why it disturbed the people of Dartmouth to take action against Great Britain and Ireland. The townspeople had not forgotten the aid sent them by Great Britain and Ireland after King Philip's War. But time had changed things!

1774 VOTE

What did Dartmouth's townspeople vote in 1774? First, they said they would not buy any goods manufactured in Great Britain and Ireland which were brought into our country. This was hard on the colonists because the English did not allow them to do any manufacturing here. One result was that the people had to wear coarse, homespun American clothes.

Why did the English forbid the colonists to engage in manufacturing? Because if the colonist didn't do any manufacturing, they would be forced to buy manufactured goods from England. England wanted to sell her goods to us. That was what a colony was supposed to be for.

Secondly, the Dartmouthites said they would not purchase any goods from any hawker or peddler. What is a hawker? Third, the voters promised not to purchase any foreign tea. Do you know what the word foreign means? Lastly, our townspeople said they would not export any flax seed to a foreign market. What is flax seed used for?

QUAKER BELIEF

Many of Dartmouth's early settlers were Quakers. The Quakers did not believe in fighting and in wars. They thought fighting and wars were wicked. They believed men should love each other and live in peace. Nevertheless, they realized they had to be prepared if war came. It seemed certain war would soon begin. Therefore, in 1775, our Quaker community voted to support the colonies in their fight against England. They also bought a supply of gunpowder and other ammunition to have in case the town needed it.

England steadfastly refused to change the laws the colonists disliked. The colonists refused to obey the laws forced on them by English government. The quarrel between them grew hotter. Eventually, England sent troops here to try to force the colonists to obey the laws. Of course, the colonists did not like that. They hated to see the English (British) soldiers in this country.

REVOLUTIONARY WAR BEGINS

The Revolutionary War began at the battle of Lexington, Massachusetts, on April 19, 1775. (Now perhaps you can understand why April 19th is called Patriot's Day.) This war was fought between four hundred trained British soldiers and seventy-seven untrained colonial soldiers called Minutemen. Every man promised to be ready to fight at a minute's notice. The Minutemen formed companies and drilled at night. (Sometime, try to go to Lexington and see the monument to these

Minutemen.) The colonies had no regular army at this time. The army was made up of volunteers. On April 21, 1775, three companies of Dartmouth men were hastily gathered and marched from our town to Roxbury (near Boston) to join the colonial army.

The battle of Bunker Hill, Massachusetts, June 17, 1775, was also important. Dartmouth men were there, too.

In 1775, the port of Boston was closed by the British as punishment for the Boston Tea Party. No goods could be brought into Boston. No goods could be shipped out of Boston. Needless to say, this law caused great hardship among the people of Boston and the surrounding areas.

These people were not forgotten by the residents of Dartmouth who appointed a committee to "… receive all the donations for the poor of Boston and Charlestown now suffering by reason of the Boston Port Bill (so called) that may be offered by the inhabitants of this town, made remittance as soon as may be to the overseer of the poor of Boston."

DARTMOUTH MEN SEE ACTION

In the first three years of the fighting, Dartmouth supplied one hundred twenty men. Actually, approximately five hundred Dartmouth men served in the army sometime during the war. Dartmouth also supplied a large number of men for the colonial navy.

Did any fighting take place in Dartmouth during the Revolutionary War? Yes, our town was invaded by the British on September 5, 1778. Let's see why the British raided Dartmouth. After all, Dartmouth was not one of the most important cities in the thirteen colonies.

The Revolutionary War interfered with some of Dartmouth's ways of earning a living, such as whaling and trading. Just before the war broke out, Dartmouth had about one hundred ships engaged in whaling and trading. This was soon stopped by the powerful English navy. About fifty of our town's whaling ships were destroyed by the British during the war. The captured sailors were given two choices. The British said, "Join a

British man-of-war (war ship) or join a British whale ship." Most captured colonial seamen preferred to join the whale ships. In this way, the British learned many of our whaling secrets.

PRIVATEERING

Remember that Britain's powerful navy soon prevented most of our whaling and trading. Of necessity, most of our ships had to be withdrawn from trade. That meant many ships were idle in Dartmouth. What were these men who worked on these ships to do? Some of them turned to privateering.

Privateering is a new word to you, isn't it? It may be a little hard for you to understand. Privateering is a war term. Privateers were ships used during the war. They were not war vessels. Instead, they were merchant (trading) ships outfitted with guns commissioned to fight by the colonial government. These privateers would try to capture enemy ships. Any ships and cargo captured belonged to the privateersmen. This made it legal so they were not pirates. If however, the English captured the privateer, the owner suffered the loss, not the colonial government under which if had been commissioned.

Privateering was a daring and dangerous thing to do, but many privateersmen made small fortunes by engaging in it. Besides, all the ships they captured or destroyed could no longer be used by the English. In that way, privateering helped the cause of the colonies.

A few of Dartmouth's residents became interested in privateering. They brought their prizes (that is what the captured ships were called) into Dartmouth's harbors, chiefly Bedford Harbor, the harbor on the Acushnet River. They unloaded their cargos there and stored them in the warehouses built along the banks of the river.

When trouble started, the British did some privateering, too. Indeed, they sometimes used Bedford Harbor. A British war sloop, the Falcon, brought two prize ships into Bedford Harbor. Leaving the two ships at the mouth of the Acushnet River under the control of some British seamen, the Falcon sailed away.

In the Fairhaven section of Old Dartmouth, there was an intensely patriotic group of men. They were organized as a militia. These men were determined to regain control of the two colonial ships seized by the British. Consequently, on May 13, they chartered the "Success," an old sloop (boat) tied up in Acushnet Harbor.

Under the leadership of Captain Daniel Egery, about twenty-five of the Fairhaven militia boarded the "Success" on a dark and foggy night. They hid below the decks. Captain Nathanial Pope was the naval officer in charge of the "Success." He piloted her out of the harbor and skillfully navigated her beside the first captured sloop. Before the British were aware of what was taking place, the Fairhaven militia had boarded the sloop and recaptured her. The British seamen aboard were taken prisoners. The captured sloop was taken into Fairhaven and anchored there.

But the Dartmouth patriots had not finished their work. It was now daylight, yet they set sail again in an effort to regain the other captured colonial slip. The Old Dartmouth militia had some keen sharpshooters. After hitting several British seamen, including a British officer, they forced the British to surrender. None of the colonists was hurt. The "Success" sailed back into the Acushnet River Harbor with the sloop and the captured British seamen. As prisoners, the British seamen were marched to jail in Taunton for safekeeping.

Thus, Dartmouth can claim credit for the first recorded sea venture in the Revolutionary War. Many of the Bedford merchants in Dartmouth were Quakers. As Quakers, they did not participate actively in the fighting. Because war had not yet actually been declared, many of these Quakers disapproved of retaining the fifteen British seamen and of marching them to Taunton for safekeeping. But the highest authority in Massachusetts at that time approved the action of the Fairhaven militia. The British sailors were kept prisoners.

Many Americans, including Dartmouth residents, were captured during the war. Some of them, especially those taken at sea, were kept in English prisons until the war ended.

Privateersmen from other towns, especially Boston and Providence, Rhode Island, also found Bedford Harbor a haven. They knew the supplies they needed could be secured here. The privateersmen felt that Bedford Harbor was a safe place to keep their prizes. Actually, Dartmouth had few ship owners who turned to privateering, but many of her men were sailors on ships engaged in privateering.

However, the British soon learned that our town contained large stores of guns, ammunition, and other war supplies. They felt it their duty to destroy the supplies concealed here. Of course, the British knew that when the colonists captured a British ship, its cargo might later be used against them in war. Therefore, they decided to take action to end the privateering here. They were determined to stop the privateersmen from using the Acushnet River as a home base.

TORY HELP

You may be thinking that not all the colonists favored gaining freedom from England. That was not the case. Although there was strong feeling in favor of separating from England, many colonists did not want to fight with England. They took England's side in this trouble.

The colonists who favored England were called Tories. Some of these Tories gave secret information to the English. In that way, the British found out the best time to attack Dartmouth. They selected a time when most of the men were absent.

Why were most of the men away from the town? The men had gone to Rhode Island to help the American army engaged in fighting there. No wonder the British decided it would be a good time to attack the town!

THE ATTACK

Early in the morning of September 5, 1778, a British squadron of about twenty vessels was sighted in Buzzard's Bay. Carrying a force of between four and five thousand men, the ships sailed into Clark's Cove. Do you know where Clark's Cove is? Soon the large ships cast anchor, boats were lowered, and the British army came ashore. Since the population of all of Dartmouth numbered only about seven thousand people at that time, this large army of British soldiers must have been frightening.

General Gray was the British leader. General Gray and his soldiers marched into the Bedford section of Old Dartmouth.

Did the British kill or harm the inhabitants as they marched through the town? No, they did not harm many people. Only three men were killed. One of these armed men fired on the British soldiers first. Immediately, the British shot the three Dartmouthites.

Actually, there were not many people in the Bedford section of Dartmouth by the time the British arrived because the townspeople had been warned of such a possibility. The first warning was a posted notice put up August 17, 1778. The notice proposed that the townspeople move food, clothing, and all other private property out into the country or some other place of safety. The notice further mentioned that the town officials would move such goods at the owner's expense if the owners wished. Many of the town's citizens heeded this early warning and had moved into the woods or some place away from the water by the time the British fleet arrived on September 5th.

Then, too, when the British were sighted, three shots were fired from Fort Phoenix (Fairhaven) to alert the townspeople. Soon after these shots were fired, the area near the waterfront was almost deserted as people fled carrying as many of their belongings as they could. Many of these fugitives found shelter in the woods. Remember, much of Dartmouth was still forested.

But we should remember that the British had not come to Dartmouth to harm the people. Their desire was to destroy the ships and the storehouses. This they soon accomplished. They set fire to practically all the boats on the Acushnet River. That meant the British destroyed about seventy ships. (One of these ships was named, "No Duty of Tea.") Most of the seventy ships were privateers, prizes, or whale ships. The British also burned about twenty shops and warehouses.

What was stored in the warehouses? A variety of supplies were stored in the warehouses including molasses, coffee, sugar, rum, tea, tobacco, cotton, gunpowder, sailcloth, cordage, and medicine.

Were any homes destroyed? Yes, about eleven houses were destroyed. These eleven houses were located along the waterfront. For the most part, only those houses near the wharves were destroyed. The wharves were burned, too. The British marched along the Acushnet River shore. That was a march of about six miles.

MAJOR ISRAEL FEARING

Next, the British moved into present-day Fairhaven. They destroyed Fort Phoenix. The British intended to treat the Fairhaven section of Old Dartmouth as they had treated Bedford. They wanted to burn the houses and buildings along the banks of the Acushnet River. The homes of several patriotic colonists were destroyed. But young Major Israel Fearing of Wareham was determined to give the British a battle in the Fairhaven section of Old Dartmouth.

Fairhaven had a spirited militia. Upon hearing of the landing of the British troops at Clark's Cove, Minutemen from the surrounding towns joined the Fairhaven militia. The colonel in command was an elderly gentleman who felt it was useless to try to fight against such a superior number of soldiers. His fear was passed on to most of the men he was leading.

But one man refused to give up so easily. That man was Major Israel Fearing. He asked for volunteers. About one hundred men offered their services. Although his men were few, they felt they could strike a blow at the enemy. Major Fearing placed his men where they could not be seen by the British. When Major Fearing noticed that the courage of some of his volunteers was wavering, he took a position in the rear and threatened to shoot any man who lost courage and tried to desert the group. His actions quieted the men and apparently gave them renewed courage, for they fired upon the British. The British made a hasty retreat, and took to their ships in the harbor. Thus, thanks to Major Fearing's splendid leadership and courage, the Fairhaven section of Old Dartmouth was spared from damage and destruction.

British soldiers attempt to burn the Akin house in Padanaram. This house is still standing on Elm Street.

PADANARAM DESTRUCTION

Perhaps you are wondering if the British came to any section of present-day Dartmouth. Yes, at the time most of the British ships sailed into Clark's Cove, a few British vessels sailed into Padanaram Harbor. They knew exactly where to go because their pilots, or guides, were two Tories. (One of these was Joe Castle. You will learn more about him later.) These two Tories had previously lived in Padanaram. Because of their strong loyalty to the British, these Tories had been forced to leave Padanaram village. Many Tories had been sent away from the colonies at the time of the Revolutionary War. I'm sure you can guess why.

The two former Dartmouth Tories felt that Mr. Elihu Akin was largely responsible for their being forced to leave Dartmouth. They wanted to get even with him.

After piloting the English ships into Padanaram Harbor, the Dartmouth Tories pointed out the property belonging to Mr. Akin. The British burned Mr. Akins's home. They burned his brother's home, too. They also attempted to burn Mr. Akins's sister's home, but were unsuccessful because of the high courage shown by the woman who lived there. She put out the fire by throwing water on it. Again, the British set fire to the house. Again, the lady extinguished the blaze. A third time the British put a torch to the house. Undaunted, the lady threw pails of water on the fire, extinguishing it and at the same time dousing some British soldiers. The disgusted British left without doing any real damage to the house, thanks to the lady's brave efforts.

The British burned a ship recently built on the shore of the Apponegansett River in Padanaram. An Akin relative was part owner of the newly constructed boat. This destruction was also a matter of getting even with the Akins.

ANOTHER ATTEMPT

This was the only time the British actually did any fighting in our town, although less than one year later, on April 2, 1778, a much smaller British squadron made an attempt to move into Bedford Harbor. However, this time they were unsuccessful. The British ships sailed away after a barrage of shots from the reconditioned Fort Phoenix made them feel they were moving into dangerous territory. Occasionally, still, our harbor was used to dock captured British ships.

Our town continued to help the other colonists in their fight for independence until the Revolutionary War ended. For instance, on October 14, 1780, it was "…voted that 1057 pounds (money) and 161 silver money be raised by way of tax on the inhabitants of said town … for purchasing the town proportion of beef sent for by the General Court to supply the Continental Army."

We can honestly say our town did its part in the Revolutionary War.

CHAPTER 9

SOME STORIES CONCERNING THE BRITISH INVASION OF DARTMOUTH

THE LADY AND THE WARMING PAN

Have you ever seen or heard of a warming pan? In colonial days, warming pans were used to heat beds. A warming pan looked like a covered frying pan with a long handle. The pan was heated by filling it with hot coals. Then it was moved around under the blankets to heat the bed. There were no furnaces to heat houses in colonial times. Therefore, a warming pan would be very useful in cold weather. After all, no one likes to get into a cold bed.

A woman who was fleeing in order to avoid being captured by the British soldiers during the British raid in the Revolutionary War, left behind all her household belongings except her brass warming pan. She was determined that she wouldn't leave the warming pan because she had had to save her money for many years in order to afford one. As she moved through the woods, the brass warming pan brushed against the branches of the trees. You can imagine what a racket that made! The other people who were fleeing with this woman felt that the noise might attract the British soldiers. They did not want to be caught by the British. They threatened to leave the woman unless she discarded her noisemaker! She refused to surrender her cherished warming pan—not after waiting years to own one! Since she would not abandon it, her companions abandoned her. Fortunately, the British did not go into the woods where she was hiding so both she and her warming pan were safe.

A DESERTER

Another story from the Revolutionary War days concerns a man named Joe Castle. He was a farm hand. He worked on the farm of Mr. Joseph Russell. Apparently, he did not care for either his job or the loyal colonists. When the British marched into Old

Dartmouth, Joe Castle decided to join them. We would call Joe Castle a Tory. Before deserting Mr. Russell's farm, Joe took a piece of chalk and wrote a message on the barn door. This was Joe Castle's message: "I make no more stone wall for old Joe Russell."

It may interest you to know that Joe Castle was forbidden to ever return to Dartmouth. Loyal Dartmouthites let it be known that Joe Castle would be unwelcome. They threatened to arrest and fine him if he ever returned to our town. Tories were not welcome in Old Dartmouth.

A STRANGE REWARD

A woman is given credit for saving a house in the present-day New Bedford section of Old Dartmouth. She was busy knitting when British soldiers entered the house in which she lived. She was not surprised as she heard they were coming. She paid no attention to them. The British soldiers took all the food from the pantry. She said nothing but kept on knitting. She very calmly continued her knitting until the soldiers set fire to the building. Then she quickly dropped her knitting and put out the fire. This happened twice. Disgusted, the British gave up and went away. When the gentlemen who owned the house heard of the woman's courage, he gave her a reward. You'll never guess what it was! It was five pounds of rice! Perhaps it was not much of a reward for such a deed, but rice may have been hard to get, or it was the woman's favorite food.

SPIC AND SPAN

Sometimes we hear a person spoken of as a "spic and span" housekeeper. What does that mean? A lady who could thus be described was cleaning her house when she was advised the British soldiers were approaching. Unafraid, she did not stop her cleaning. Her neighbors, who were hastily preparing to depart, tried to get her to accompany them. This she refused to do. Instead, she remarked, "If the enemy comes to my house, they shall find it in good order." What would you have done if you found yourself in a similar situation?

A TEMPTING MEAL

What favorite New England food is considered ideal for Saturday night's supper? Did you know it was pork and beans? At one home in Old Dartmouth, some loaves of bread, pork, and beans had already been put into the oven in preparation for a meal (breakfast). When the occupants of the house heard the British were coming, they fled without waiting for their food. Can you guess the ending of the story? The aroma was so tempting you could hardly blame the British soldiers for partaking of such a delicious meal.

A PATRIOTIC COLONIST

The British came prepared to burn the home of Mr. Bartholomew West, a very patriotic colonist who lived in present-day Fairhaven. When the British arrived, they announced they were going to burn the West home. Mr. West, an elderly and sickly gentleman, was ill in bed at that time. Mr. West was not able to leave the house by his own power because he was so weak. His housekeeper asked the British soldiers to carry him to safety. This they refused to do. Whereupon the determined housekeeper lifted Mr. West out of bed and promptly carried him outside to safety. She didn't lack courage, did she? Although Mr. West's life was spared, his home was completely destroyed. That was the price he paid for his devotion to the colonies.

A HASTY EXIT IN VAIN

A story is told about Miss Betsy Tinkham. Miss Tinkham happened to be at Clark's Cove when the British fleet arrived on September 5th. She didn't live at Clark's Cove, but was there attending a wedding. When she saw the British boats approaching, she hastily departed from the wedding. She ran all the way home (corner of Union Street and Acushnet Avenue). Her first thought was to save some of her valuables. But where to put them? She finally decided the best place would be on her boat in the Acushnet River. There they could be floated up the river. Surely, they would be safe there! But as you know, the British burned practically all the craft on the Acushnet River and Miss Tinkham's boat was no exception. Miss Tinkham herself was not harmed. She escaped to the woods, but she lost her most cherished possessions.

EXTRA TROUSERS

Our next little incident tells of the clever use Jonathan Kempton made of an extra pair of trousers. When Mr. Kempton heard of the approach of the British troops in Dartmouth, he hurried to his home. He quickly tossed a few valuables into a small trunk. Seeking to have extra clothing, he donned a second pair of trousers over the trousers he was already wearing. But, alas, he had lingered too long! As he was dashing out of his home, he was met by a couple of British soldiers. They promptly seized both Mr. Kempton and his trunk. As several soldiers set fire to some bedding in the house, Mr. Kempton was placed under the supervision of one guard. This guard immediately started to march him to the waterfront. In trying to help himself to Mr. Kempton's watch, the guard discovered that his prisoner was wearing two pair of trousers. Mr. Kempton was quick-witted. He bargained with the guard, "If you let me go free, I'll give you this extra pair of trousers." The solider must have figured he had nothing to lose and he probably thought an extra pair of trousers might come in handy. At any rate, the bargain was made and carried out, whereupon Mr. Kempton hastily rushed home. Once there, he found the other British soldiers had departed. Mr. Kempton was able to put out the fire and save his house. He was lucky.

JOHN PAUL JONES

John Paul Jones is recognized as one of our country's outstanding naval heroes. He captured more prizes than any other privateersman.

Mr. Jones came to America from the country of Scotland in the year 1773. When our Continental Congress created a navy in the year 1775, John Paul Jones offered his services. In recognition of his great ability, the Continental Congress appointed him senior lieutenant.

While doing fine service along our North Atlantic coast, Jones frequently visited the Acushnet River Harbor in Dartmouth. Many of his crew were Dartmouth men.

Once while fighting a British brig-of-war which was much superior in gun power to Jones' "Providence," Jones used old bolts, spikes, and other pieces of scrap iron found about the ship in his guns. It proved effective causing much damage to the British ship. The British surrendered. Jones brought his prize into Dartmouth's Bedford Harbor. Many of the dead seamen from this battle are buried in Old Dartmouth.

THE "BEDFORD"

It may surprise you to learn that a Dartmouth ship was the first to fly the American flag in foreign waters. This ship was named the "Bedford." It sailed to England with a load of whale oil. The Bedford arrived in England in February 1783 on the day the treaty of peace ending the Revolutionary War was signed. The Bedford was the first American ship to fly the American flag with thirteen stripes. (What do these thirteen stripes stand for?)

LAFAYETTE

Do you remember that in the preceding story you learned that the country of France aided us greatly in the Revolutionary War? One Frenchman, Lafayette, was outstanding in the assistance he gave our country. Lafayette came all the way across the Atlantic Ocean from France to help us. He used some of his own money to buy supplies for us. Lafayette worked very closely with General George Washington, the first president of the United States. Washington loved Lafayette and treated him like a son.

At one time during the Revolutionary War, Lafayette was stationed close to Dartmouth in the town of Warren, Rhode Island. He was the commander of the American troops that were there. Once, he rode his horse through our town. He was riding at the head of his troops. That was the year 1778. You will read more about Lafayette when you are older. But don't forget that this famous Frenchman, who loved liberty as we do, once passed through our town.

Did you enjoy these little stories about the Revolutionary War?

In early Dartmouth the boys worked hard.

CHAPTER 10

EDUCATION

The chief goal of education has always been to develop young people into better citizens so they will be able to take their place as adults in the community. The First Americans who lived in this country educated their children—not by sending them to school, but by teaching them the skills that would help them to obtain enough food and to protect themselves when they became adults.

What kind of an education did the early white settlers in America need? Most of them were farmers so the boys were taught to be good farmers. The girls were trained to be good future housewives and mothers. The early pioneer children received most of their education in their own homes.

EDUCATION OF A COLONIAL BOY

From his father, a boy learned to make shovels, knives, plows, sleds, carts, wagons, brooms, baskets, and wooden bowls. He made wooden handles for axes, hoes, spades, and pitchforks. He learned how to build fences, houses, and barns. Farmers cut their hay and wheat with sickles and scythes in those days. You can be sure that was hard work since it was all done by hand and muscle. From his father, the colonial boy learned how to use the sickle and scythe. The boy in the family helped with the planting and worked out in the field. He learned to make shoes from the hides of animals. That was the kind of education he needed when our country was an infant colonial settlement.

A COLONIAL GIRL'S EDUCATION

The girl's education was not neglected either. She learned homemaking skills while very young. Remember, all clothes were made at home then. The amount of cloth needed for the family kept the girls and their mother very, very busy. Making cloth was slow, tiresome work. The girl had to learn how to comb wool, spin it into thread, and then weave it into cloth. She needed to know these skills in order to help the family, and also so she could take care of her own family when she married. As she grew older, the girl started making the linen she would need after marriage. The young lady learned how to embroider and knit.

There were no electric or gas stoves then. The food had to be cooked in pots at the big fireplace. Pots were hung over the open fire on an iron rod called a crane. The crane was fastened to the side of the fireplace. Cooking was a skill girls learned early in life. They knew how to make butter and cheese for they could not go to the store to buy any. They learned how to salt and pickle meat so there would be meat for the long winter months. The girls had to know how to make candles for candles furnished the needed light. Do you know what a mold is? Perhaps your mother used a mold for making jello. When making candles, the girls and women poured hot wax or fat into molds of tin and iron.

Thus, you can see the children who lived in this country in colonial days worked very hard to get an education even though most of them never attended a regular school. For the most part, their entire day was spent in work.

EARLY LAWS

An early colonial law in Massachusetts fixed a fine of ten pounds on any town not hiring schoolmasters (as teachers were called then). Later, when it was discovered that many towns were neglecting to hire a teacher, the General Court of Massachusetts increased the penalty to twenty pounds. (If a pound was worth $4.00, how much did these penalties amount to?)

Although the General Court passed a law saying that each town must have a teacher, no law was passed to say that boys and girls must go to school. In fact, attending school was considered a luxury. That was partly because a parent had to pay a certain sum of money if his child attended school. Generally speaking, most children who lived on farms never attended school.

Dipping candles was one of the chores for girls in early Dartmouth. Notice the big fireplace.

Only boys went to school in those days. It was considered a waste of time and unnecessary for girls to go to school.

THE FIRST SCHOOLS

We usually think of schools when we talk about education. The first mention of a formal educational system in Dartmouth can be found in the town meeting records of July 7, 1702. The records contain the following report: "At a town meeting the 7th day of July 1702 it was agreed forty pounds (English money) for the paying of our Schoolmaster, 18 pounds for a years schooling."

Mr. Daniel Shepherd was the first Dartmouth teacher mentioned by name. The 1711 minutes (report) of the Dartmouth Friends (Quakers) tells us that there were no schoolhouses at first. Instead, lessons were taught in someone's home: "Daniel Shepherd of Shepherd Plains, not far from here toward the Tucker road, taught a school in John Russell's home near the present Town Hall."

Many of the early teachers were also ministers. The ministers were the best-educated people. This was true in most New England colonies.

Evidence that early Dartmouth teachers boarded out is noted for the first time in April 1728, when it "Voted that Josiah Mayhew shall have forty shillings for boarding, William Palmer, the town schoolmaster."

SUBJECTS TAUGHT

By 1727, more than one teacher was needed. Town records state, "Voted that there shall be suitable schoolmasters to teach the children to read, write, and cypher." (Cypher means arithmetic.)

In the early 1700s, schools were kept only four months of the year. However, the teacher often taught all year, but in three different sections of the town.

Since geographically Dartmouth commanded the northwest portion of Buzzard's Bay, many of its men became interested in fishing and shipbuilding.

Usually the very early schools offered only three subjects: reading, writing, and arithmetic. But because so many men were interested in the sea, perhaps it is not surprising that navigation was one subject offered in the Dartmouth schools in 1735. (What does navigation refer to?) Those who studied navigation had to pay extra money for the lessons. Surveying was also taught for those interested. (What does surveying mean? Why might a knowledge of surveying be useful?)

SCHOOL DISTRICTS

From 1798 to 1866, all Massachusetts towns were by law divided into various school districts.

From earliest time until 1826, the town selectmen had the power to hire and dismiss teachers. In 1826, the state passed a law establishing school committees. Every town had to have one. The school committee took over the job of hiring and dismissing teachers. Usually Dartmouth's school committee consisted of three members. These members were generally chosen from as near as possible to the three corners of the town: Smith Mills, Russells Mills, and Padanaram. That seemed the fairest way. Each member was supposed to supervise the school district closest to his home. It was the duty of the school committee members to visit the district schools to examine the progress of the pupils.

It was the custom for the teachers to board with the different families of the district. The usual arrangement was for the schoolmaster to stay a few days, a week, or possibly longer with one family and then move on to another. The family sending the most children to school boarded the teacher for the longest period. This constant moving about in boarding places must have been hard on the teachers.

DARTMOUTH'S FIRST PUBLIC SCHOOLHOUSE

All records seem to indicate that the first public schoolhouse in our town was built at the head of Gulf Road, also known as Seth David Corner (near Motha Square) in South Dartmouth. This first schoolhouse was a small one-room building. It was situated by the side of the highway so that the door opened directly onto the road. Apparently, the highway served as a play area when needed. It was reasonably safe at that time because there were no cars or buses on the roads then. (It was the custom to build the schoolhouse just off the road.) John Greenleaf Whittier, one of America's greatest posts, wrote a poem which begins thus:

"Still sits the school house by the road."

It is a lovely poem. You will enjoy reading it when you are older.

THE SCHOOLS

Some of these early schools were quite small. Let us read the measurements of a one-room school built in Dartmouth over a century and three quarters ago. (How long is that?)

"The floor is 15 feet 8 inches by 15 feet 4 inches. The height of the room was 7 feet 8 inches, and there was formerly a little entry 3 feet 8 inches in width."

This building held up to sixty children. How crowded it must have been! Maybe your teacher will let you measure your schoolroom some day. You may feel your room is overcrowded, but I'm sure you don't have anywhere near that number of children in your room.

Neither time nor money was spent in decorating Dartmouth's first schoolhouse. The pupils were seated on long backless benches. These benches were usually placed on three sides of the room. Backless benches must have been very uncomfortable after a while.

The teacher had a high, sloping desk at the front of the room. He sat on a high stool so he could keep a sharp eye on all his students.

There might be a chair or two in the room to be used by the visiting school committee or other visitors.

Neither the inside nor the outside of the building was painted. It must have been somewhat gloomy. There were no blackboards, outline maps, or globes. The teacher and pupils had little to work with. The pupils wrote on slates with a slate pencil. They used a cloth as an eraser.

The schools were heated by large stoves. Students were expected to supply the wood. Those who sat near the stove were likely to be uncomfortably hot. Those who sat at a distance from the stove were very cold. Aren't you glad we have such bright, comfortable, roomy schools now?

COMPARISON OF EARLY AND PRESENT-DAY SCHOOLS

In what other ways did these early schools differ from ours? Here are some ways those schools were unlike our schools. The old schools were all one-room buildings. We do not have any one-room schools in Dartmouth now. These early schools were ungraded. Dartmouth schools today are graded. Some very young children attended school in the 1700s and 1800s. Just imagine some children were only two years old while others were as old as eighteen years. What a wide range of ages the teacher had to work with in the same room! Now, girls and boys have to be almost five years old before they can enter school to attend kindergarten. We do not have teenagers in the same room as our youngest children. All children in a classroom are about the same age.

The early schools had no playgrounds. Very little time was allotted for play, anyway. Today's schools have larger playgrounds where the younger boys and girls can get together and have fun several times a day.

Until the year 1848, school met everyday but Sunday. When schools were in session, the teachers had to teach on July 4th, Thanksgiving Day, and Christmas. We would think it strange if we went to school on these days, wouldn't we?

Dartmouth's first schoolhouse.

Until a century ago, each pupil supplied his own textbook. At the present time, the town supplies us with our books. Each classroom is equipped with multi-textbooks. There is a much greater selection of books today. The books of long ago did not include the beautiful color illustrations our books of today contain. These illustrations help us to make our books more interesting and help us to picture what we read.

How our schools have grown! From one teacher in 1702, we now have 315 teachers and 22 administrators. No longer do we have dark, poorly ventilated schools. The schools in Dartmouth are colorfully painted to create a pleasant environment. Also, Dartmouth schools are equipped and planned to give the best possible education. We have a wide selection of books and all kinds of supplies and audio-visual equipment. Our furniture is comfortable, too. In one of our earliest high school graduating classes (in the late 1800s), there were six students. Today there are 3988 students. In the year 1961, there were 156 in the graduating class of the Dartmouth High School. In June 1975, 308 graduates, and in 2010, 267 graduates. There are far more curriculum offerings in high school today. Also, we have music, art, and physical education supervisors who work closely with the students and teachers. We have learning disability teachers to work with individuals and small groups who have learning problems.

Another sign of growth in our educational system is that today every boy and girl attends school. Boys and girls have the opportunity to attend school until they are at least sixteen years old. The law says attendance is compulsory to the age of sixteen. Today the vast majority remain one or two more years and attain a high school diploma.

Our educational system has broadened in many ways.

CHAPTER 11

HENRY H. CRAPO

When we say someone is "famous" what do we mean? Can we say the President of the United States is famous? Can we call the governor of our state famous? This story is about a Dartmouth teacher who became famous. His name was Henry H. Crapo.

BOYHOOD

Henry H. Crapo was born in Dartmouth on May 24, 1804. His father made only a modest living as a farmer. As a boy, Henry worked hard on the farm.

Henry had little opportunity to go to school but he was possessed of the same thirst for knowledge as our great presidents, Andrew Johnson and Abraham Lincoln. Like Johnson and Lincoln, Henry was largely self-educated. He loved to read. He read all the books he could find. He kept a little notebook in which he wrote down the new words he found in the books. What he really did was to make his own little dictionary. In the process, he improved his vocabulary tremendously.

A SURVEYOR

Henry did not wish to devote his life to farming. At that time, there was a demand for surveyors. Henry decided to become a surveyor. To learn this skill, he read a book on surveying. But a surveyor needed a compass. Henry did not own a compass. He had no money to buy one. That did not stop him. He decided to make a compass. He secured permission from a neighboring blacksmith to make a compass out of some scrap iron owned by the blacksmith. (What is a blacksmith? Why were there so many blacksmiths then?) Henry worked on his compass in the blacksmith's shop using the forge while the blacksmith was at dinner. After he finished making his compass, Mr. Crapo was ready to earn money surveying. As a surveyor, Mr. Crapo measured and diagrammed the land.

COUNTRY SCHOOLMASTER

Henry Crapo planned to earn some money in another way, too. He decided to become a teacher. Why did he want to be a teacher? Mr. Crapo wanted to be a teacher because he thought teaching was the best way to learn and improve his own knowledge.

At the age of seventeen, he applied for a district teaching position and was hired "on trial." He did so well he became a regular teacher. Mr. Crapo worked very hard as a teacher. Like all good teachers, he took a personal interest in his students. He taught school for nearly ten years in Dartmouth, Westport, and Tiverton, Rhode Island.

A district teacher's salary was then uncertain. The parents had to be persuaded to pay a small amount of money for their children's tuition. This money was difficult to collect at times. The following is a note kept by Mr. Crapo:

"Howard Potter Dr. to Henry H. Crapo, March 21st, 1827 to 14 6/11 weeks tuition at 25c = $3.64. Cr. by 1 cord wood at 21 = $3.50. Balance $0.14. Received payment, Henry H. Crapo." (Perhaps your teacher will explain what Dr. stands for in this case. What did this parent use for payment? How much money did Mr. Crapo actually receive?) Remember this was payment for one pupil's school year.

At this time, there was some talk about establishing a high school in Dartmouth. Mr. Crapo desired to teach in the high school, but felt that his lack of formal schooling might prove to be a handicap. However, Mr. Crapo was not one to sit back and do nothing. He walked to New Bedford, a fourteen-mile roundtrip distance from his home. Once there, he asked John Page, Master of the private school, Friend's Academy, (Friend's Academy was located in New Bedford for many years before moving to Tucker Road, Dartmouth) to give him a test to discover whether he was adequately prepared to teach in a high school. Mr. Crapo easily passed the test. He was thrilled when

Mr. Page gave him a certificate indicating he was qualified to teach high school.

Mr. Crapo became our first high school teacher. He kept a notebook during a nineteen-week teaching session in the high school. This notebook reveals many interesting details concerning a teacher's life in those days.

A TEACHER'S LIFE

For example, Mr. Crapo boarded at thirty-five different places. His longest time in one place was seven days, two meals. His shortest stopover was one day.

During twelve of the nineteen months, he taught school six days weekly. He taught five and one-half days a week for three weeks. Only for four weeks did he have a five-day week such as we have now. Mr. Crapo was paid $18.00 monthly.

LIFE IN MICHIGAN

Because he thought he might make a better living for his family of ten children, Mr. Crapo moved to the state of Michigan.

In Michigan, Mr. Crapo bought large amounts of woodlands. He became one of the most successful lumbermen in the state.

Additionally, he had several model farms stocked with high-grade animals. Here he became nationally famous. Henry H. Crapo was elected governor of Michigan.

At Mr. Crapo's death, a fellow worker said, "Michigan never had a governor before who devoted as much personal attention and pains taking labor to his public duties as did he."

What wonderful praise for this Dartmouth native and former teacher!

THE CRAPO GIFT

When Mr. Crapo's wife, Mary Ann Slocum Crapo, passed away in 1876, she left $3000 to our town. The money was to be used to promote the welfare of boys and girls in Dartmouth schools. In appreciation of Mrs. Crapo's generosity, Dartmouth later honored her by calling the elementary school on Slocum Road near the town hall the Mary A. Crapo School. The Crapo School is no longer standing. One purchase with money from the Crapo Fund was the audiometer. Another purchase was a vision-testing machine. The audiometer and vision-testing machine were used for many years for the benefit of all Dartmouth children!

The Crapos unquestionably merit recognition in our town's history. If you work as hard as Mr. Crapo did, perhaps your name will also go down in Dartmouth's history — so aim high!

Shipbuilding At Old Dartmouth

CHAPTER 12

SHIPBUILDING IN DARTMOUTH

Have you ever stood on the Padanaram Bridge and watched the boats sailing in and out of the harbor? As they come and go, they make an interesting, colorful picture.

Wouldn't it be fun to see a boat grow from a mere frame to a finished product of great beauty? The boys and girls living in Dartmouth a century ago saw many ship's keels laid. Some of them watched as the ship was being built. This may have attracted many boys to the seafaring life for many of the men of Dartmouth in the past were sailors.

Dartmouth turned to shipbuilding for Dartmouth had lumber (trees) to use in building ships, rivers on which to build and float the boats, and men to do the work. In Dartmouth, men cut oak, cedar, pine, and spruce trees from the forests to use in building fishing and sailing vessels. Oak was the most common kind of wood used, primarily for the hulls. Cedar, pine, and spruce were used for the masts and yards.

In what sections of Dartmouth was shipbuilding carried on? The most natural place to build ships is on the shores of bays and harbors, or on the banks of rivers where they can be easily launched.

Most every river mouth in Dartmouth was a site for shipbuilding. In the New Bedford section of Old Dartmouth, we know that shipbuilding began as early as 1761 when Benjamin Taber moved here from Nantucket and started making ships on the shores of the Acushnet River. He built the first whaleboat in this area. Other builders soon followed Mr. Taber.

NEW ENGLAND SHIPBUILDING

New England was one of the leading ship building centers in the colonies. New England ships were busily engaged carrying goods for the other colonies as well as for themselves. The ship captains of the New England states were not only good sailors but excellent traders.

THE ROTCH FAMILY

Joseph Rotch, one of New Bedford's founders, was the first person to carry on a large and prosperous shipbuilding industry here. Mr. Rotch moved to the Bedford section of Dartmouth from the Island of Nantucket in 1765. Under Mr. Rotch's leadership, the Bedford waterfront became a very busy place. The harbor was the busiest place in town. Ship after ship was built under his direction. Some of these ships were used in whaling, but Mr. Rotch also built merchant vessels. Merchant ships carry on trade by bringing goods from one place to another.

The first large merchant vessel was built here by Mr. Rotch's son, Francis Rotch. It was called the "The Dartmouth." You became acquainted with "The Dartmouth" when you read the story of the Boston Tea Party.

SHIPBUILDING IN PADANARAM

We do not know the exact date when shipbuilding started in the Padanaram section of Old Dartmouth, but we do know some shipbuilding was carried on there in the 1700s. Do you remember that when the British invaded Old Dartmouth in 1778 they burned a ship that had just been built on the Apponegansett River? Therefore, we know some ships were being built and outfitted in Padanaram more than 200 years ago.

As early as 1750 a few whaling ships were being built on the Apponegansett River. This business remained at South Dartmouth for only ten years when the owner moved it to the Bedford section of Dartmouth because he felt the Acushnet River formed a better harbor for such an undertaking.

During the Revolutionary War, shipbuilding in this area was almost at a standstill. But by the 1820s sailing vessels, fishing boats, and whalers were again being built and launched from shipyards on the shores of the Apponegansett River in Padanaram. At least three different companies built ships there.

About the year 1826 or 1827 two gentlemen, Charles Matthews and Mathew Thatcher, started to build ships in South

Dartmouth. Theirs was not the only shipyard on the Apponegansett River.

Mr. Daniel Homer also had a shipyard in Padanaram. What a busy place Padanaram Harbor must have been at that time!

In the middle of the nineteenth century, four other men started to build large whaling ships in Padanaram. These men were Alonzo Matthews, John Mashow, James M. Babbitt, and Frederick Smalley. They continued to build ships until 1858. During that time, they built about thirty-five ships. One of these was a bark named "Henry H. Crapo." (Do you remember What Henry Crapo did?) A bark is squared rigged on the two forward masts.

SHIPBUILDING IN RUSSELLS MILLS

Some, but not much, shipbuilding was carried on in another place in Dartmouth. Ships were built in Russells Mills just below the village on the Slocum River. Because the river was shallow, the larger ships had to be floated down the Slocum River buoyed up by barrels. There is an interesting poem written about a whale ship that was fitted out at Russells Mills. It is entitled, "Grandfather's Pocketbook." After you have read it, try to think of the story it tells.

GRANDFATHER'S POCKETBOOK

Grandfather's pocketbook, faded and old!
Years three score and ten have over it rolled
Since the day and the hour when it was new,
And the sheen on it wore its glossiest hue.
Now tis gray with the touch of time's mouldy fingers,
The hard prints of which on it still lingers.
Tis made of morocco, once shining and red; —
Grandfather bought it the day he was wed!
He looked on its contents with little less pride
Than he gazed on his fair, his beautiful bride;
For that he well knew would keep want from the door,

And a welcome would give to the weary and sore.
Tis a joy to gaze on this pocketbook old —
With its cavernous cells for silver and gold;
It brings to our thoughts the time far away
When these were plenty as the scrip of today.
When sovereigns and guineas of genuine gold;
And great silver dollars were made in a mold.
Look! Here's a letter, all blotted with tears,
Yellow with age, and stained by the years;
Tis a love letter and reads much the same
As letters of this day of a similar name;
It begins with "My Darling," and tells of a love
Earnest as that of the angels above,
Tis directed to grandmother, her maiden name,
And there seems to be in it a shadow of blame
That their wedding day is so far away.
(Tis just a year from the date to the day)
It says: From Cape Cod to Boston he rode in a stage —
And grandfather's name at the end of the page.
And here's a lock of grandfather's hair!
As curling and black, as shining and fair,
As when grandmother's scissors it cut from his head,
On his twenty-first birthday, when he lovingly said, —
"Take, Susan, I pray, the whole of my head."
And that was the way he asked her to wed.
Here's their marriage certificate, crumpled and torn.
See where twas folded, how it is worn!
Twas the year eighteen hundred and the ink was wet,
Just two years from the time my grandparents met;
When they to each other gave heart to heart,
To cherish and love till death should them part.
A sailor was grandfather, brace hearted and bold,
And fearless of danger as I have been told;
Energetic and active, to all ports he went,
And short was the time that at home he spent,
But sweet were the hours there that he passed,
Though the shadow of parting was over it cast.

He sailed out of Dartmouth, one bleak winter's morning,
Just as the Break of day was first dawning.
Grandmother's lips he touched with a kiss,
And he gave her the pocketbook, saying, "Take this.
There's enough for whatever you'll want to buy —
Take care of the babies, and dearest, good bye!"
Of that vessel and crew not the slightest word,
From that day to this has ever been heard.
Grandmother waited, year out and year in,
Till her hair turned gray and her eyes grew dim;
But the lover came not, her sad heart to cheer,
Nor tiding of him e'er did she hear.
But one night in a dream as she quietly slept,
Grandfather came in and over her wept.
Over her leaned, his clothes dripping wet,
And told her then, that his sun had set;
In his face, icy cold, distinctly she read
That his body forever and ever was dead.
Time brought to grandmother offers of marriage,
A house in town and a handsome carriage;
But to each and to all grandmother said — "Nay!
In patience I'll wait till the coming bright day,
When the mansion in heaven is ready for me,
And the face of my husband again I shall see."
And now she has gone at eighty odd years,
To the home that she yearned for thro' misty tears,
And I think of the meeting on that other side
Of grandfather's greeting his long ago bride.
And I wonder, if there the perfect joy given
Compensates for the happiness here that was riven.
The babies, two boys, are old men now,
And silver hair crosses each furrowed brow;
Father and grandfather each have become,
And their journey on earth almost is done;
But thro' life's evening shadows a fair white hand
Beckons them on to the Better Land.
Grandfather's pocketbook faded and old!

Its leaves in reverence I tenderly fold,
And lay its treasures back in their place,
Putting them up in the old-fashioned case;
For, mid the choicest things I have and hold
Is grandfather's pocketbook, faded and old!

Did you like the poem? Why?

PAUL CUFFE

When we think of shipbuilding on the Westport River, we think of Paul Cuffe (or Cuffee). Mr. Cuffe, of black and Wampanoag ancestry, was born in Cuttyhunk in 1759. He attended school very little. A very smart man, he was mostly self-taught. He taught himself to read and write. He also studied mathematics and navigational skills, which were very important for a seaman or sea captain.

Paul's father bought a farm. Paul had to work very hard, for farming is not easy work. Soon Paul's father died. He left the farm to Paul and to John, Paul's older brother. For three years, from age thirteen to sixteen, Paul stayed home to help support his mother and his three younger sisters.

But, Paul Cuffe really wanted to go to sea. He became a seaman and sailed out of Bedford Harbor several times on a whaler. In 1776, during the Revolutionary War, the ship Cuffe was on was captured by the English (British). The British imprisoned Cuffe and the other sailors for three or four months in New York on a prison hulk. Then the prisoners were granted permission to return home. Paul returned to his family farm.

In 1779, John and Paul Cuffe decided to go into the trading business. They needed a vessel so they built one on the Westport River. When the small vessel was completed, the Cuffes started trading, first with Cuttyhunk and the area around Dartmouth, then with Rhode Island. Soon the Cuffes were trading as far away as Long Island Sound. Paul's trading business continued to expand. Paul, by now, had several ships. His ships carried such things as foodstuff, animals, and lumber.

Cod was the principal cargo. Cuffe's fishing ships carried codfish back to Westport where it was cleaned, salted, dried, and then packed in barrels to be shipped away, usually to the South and to the West Indies. Cuffe's trading activities made him wealthy. His ships really sailed "the seven seas." You might like to know one of Cuffe's ships was the first American ship to have an all African-American crew.

There was no schoolhouse close by his home for children to attend so Cuffe paid for the construction of a schoolhouse on his own property. He hired a teacher and paid his salary in addition to all the other expenses of maintaining the school. Children, both black and white, living in the neighborhood had the privilege of attending school without paying tuition since Mr. Cuffe paid all the expenses.

At that time free black people, even though they might pay taxes, were denied the right to vote. Cuffe worked hard to attain voting rights for free blacks. He was unsuccessful in having the law passed in Dartmouth. Yet, he wrote the petition which brought about the change in the law. In 1783, a law was passed that gave any Massachusetts taxpayer the right to vote.

Cuffe sailed to Sierra Leone on the West Coast of Africa several times and did some trading there. While visiting the English Colony for free blacks in Sierra Leone, Cuffe began to feel that America needed a similar type place for its free blacks. He started to correspond with President James Madison about his concern. Later the two men met to discuss the idea. President Madison agreed with Cuffe, but pointed out it that it would be necessary to wait for the War of 1812 to be over before taking any action.

Cuffe died in 1817 and did not live to see his dream become a reality, but a few years later, in 1822, Liberia was established as a home for black Americans in Africa. However, Cuffe lived long enough to accomplish many things that made living conditions better for African Americans. What an interesting life he had! Can you find Sierra Leone on the map of the world?

COMPANION INDUSTRIES

Wherever shipbuilding was going on, coopering was also done. Coopering refers to the making of barrels. The man who did this work was referred to as a cooper. The cooper was really an important man. Many barrels were needed, not only for home use, but also because most of the things that were shipped at that time were shipped in barrels. Boxes and buckets were sometimes used, but barrels were most frequently used. The barrels were wooden barrels. The large boards were used in building ships. The smaller boards were used for barrels, boxes, or buckets. The large barrels could hold many things. For example, the early settlers smoked, salted, or pickled and then packed their beef and pork into barrels. What meat they didn't need was shipped out of the country to be sold elsewhere. Barrels were also used on fishing boats to hold salted fish. Flour was packed in barrels, as well as cider, rum, and water. Barrels were utilized to hold food and drink for long voyages.

In Dartmouth, one could see coopers at work close by any shipyard. You might say the two businesses went hand in hand.

In those days, none of the ships had motors. They were all sailing ships. Therefore, sail making could also be found in the same area where shipbuilding was carried on. These sail-making places were, and still are, called sail lofts.

Much rope and cordage was needed to provide for the standing and running rigging, anchor hawsers, and mooring cable. Rope and cordage was made in the ropewalks in Dartmouth. The hemp to make the rope was brought into the town by merchant ships. Rope makers were kept busy making rope for the ships.

Wherever ships were being built blacksmiths were seen. They made the nails, anchors, and other hardware for the ships. Blacksmiths also made iron pots, tools, and iron shoes for the oxen and horses in the town.

Shipbuilding created many jobs because it took all kinds of workers such as lumbermen, ships' carpenters, blacksmiths, sail makers, rope makers, and coopers. Of course, sailors were also needed. Like all shipbuilding towns, Dartmouth was a very busy place.

There is a sail loft on the waterfront in Padanaram now, located on Elm Street near the Yacht Club. There, Ike Manchester and his son make sails and ship them all over the world. Perhaps you could ask one of the men who work there to come to school to talk to you sometime. No doubt, he could tell you some interesting things about sail making. Remember, the making of sails is a skill which dates from the early history of our town and contributed much to our Dartmouth heritage.

CHAPTER 13

WHALING

What does the expression "There (Thar) she blows" mean to you? Read this story and you will find out what "There (Thar) she blows" meant to Dartmouthites for well over a century in the town's history.

From the earliest times, Dartmouth men were interested in fishing. That's not surprising since the town is located on the shores of Buzzards Bay. You might say the sea was at our doorstep. Local fishermen caught many cod, herring, and mackerel. They sailed out of Dartmouth's harbors in their sturdy boats. Sometimes they used hooks to catch fish, but more often large nets were used. Later the nets were lifted or pulled in. How happy the fishermen were when the nets were full!

As early as 1750, Dartmouth seamen were interested in a new kind of fishing. What was this new kind of fishing? This new kind of fishing was the catching of whales, or whaling, as it is usually called.

WHAT ARE WHALES?

Whales are not fish, even though they live in the ocean. Whales are really very large animals. Whales are the biggest animals that ever lived on this earth.

Whales are mammals, and so are we. Have you a pet? Dogs, cats, and horses are mammals, too. Mammals are warm-blooded animals. That means that their blood stays the same temperature all the time. Except on very hot summer days, our bodies are warmer than our surroundings. Fish are cold-blooded creatures. That means their blood temperature changes as the temperature of the water around them changes.

Real fish have gills by which they breathe. Like all mammals, whales breathe by the means of lungs. They breathe oxygen by means of their lungs. That means whales have to come to the surface every so often in order to breathe. While underwater, whales have to hold their breath just as we do when

A whale ship

we swim below the surface. However, whales can hold their breath much longer than people can, but, just like us, they will drown if they stay under water too long.

THE VALUE OF THE WHALE

Why were these whales so valuable? The bodies of whales were useful in many ways.

Whales have a very large amount of fat under their skin. This fat is called blubber. The thick blubber, which is between the whale's skin and flesh, helps to keep him warm.

There was much clear oil in the whale's head, especially the sperm whale's head. More oil was obtained from each whale by boiling down the blubber. When burned, whale oil gave a good light. A kind of wax was secured from the head of the whale also. It was used to make candles, which were in great demand in those days even though whale oil lamps became popular. Of course, there was no electricity then to take the place of candles or oil burning lamps. Since the whale was so valuable, many men were willing to risk their lives in the dangerous business of capturing whales.

WHALING VESSELS

Whaling vessels were large sailing vessels. If you want to see what a whaling vessel looked like, visit the Whaling Museum in New Bedford. There you can see the Bark Lagoda, a model of a whale ship. This model is one-half the size of a real whaler. The Lagoda is the largest ship model in the world and is exact in every detail. A study of the model Lagoda will help you to picture the whaling ships that put to sea from this area. Better yet, visit one of the last old sailing ships in existence, the Charles Morgan, berthed at Old Mystic Seaport in Connecticut.

Each 120 foot long whaler was equipped with several smaller boats. For what were these smaller boats used? Imagine a whaler was out to sea. Suddenly a member of the crew, the lookout man, whose post was high up in the mast of the ship, sighted a whale. Even though it might be far away he could tell it was a whale by a geyser-like spray he spotted when the whale came up to breathe. Immediately, he told of his discovery by crying out, "There she blows!"

Quickly, members of the crew lowered some of these small open boats called whale boats. Usually, the strongest and most courageous men went out in these small boats. There were at least six men in each small boat. The men rowed hard until they were close to the whale. In the meantime, the whale went below the surface. But remember, as mammals, whales have to come to the surface every so often in order to breathe. As soon as the whale again came to the surface to breathe, and was close enough, the harpooner of the whale boat threw a harpoon into the whale.

A harpoon looked like a spear. It was a long pointed iron with a head like a fishhook — once in the whale's body, he could not free himself of it easily.

The harpoon had a one thousand, three hundred foot rope attached to it. Sometimes, the injured whale put up a tremendous fight. It would swim around, gamely and excitedly, trying to get rid of its pursuer. As the whale swam, it frequently pulled the small boat after it for miles. This was called a "Nantucket sleigh ride." Whales frequently attacked the boats and sometimes smashed them into pieces. A whale could smash a boat with a single blow of its powerful tail, or its flukes. Some types of whales might even crush the boat between their powerful jaws. Another whale boat was usually close enough to pick up the crew of the smashed boat.

Thus, we see whaling was exciting, and dangerous, too. It called for fearless, strong men — men who thought it a challenge to conquer the biggest mammals to inhabit the earth!

THE KILL

But the whale was not yet dead. When the whale seemed to have tired and lost strength, the men in the small boat would quietly and quickly row up to the side of the whale. Then the ship's mate would thrust a lance into the whale's lung to kill him. Again, this was a dangerous time for the whale would fight for his life. Sometimes in the final struggle for his life, the whalers lost their own lives.

GETTING THE OIL

When the whale was dead, it was towed to the whale ship by the rope attached to the harpoon. There was a boom on the deck of the whaler. It was lowered, and then the whale was tied with rope to the side of the ship. The blubber was cut and stripped off while the whale was still floating in the water at the side of the ship. It was peeled off the whale in chunks. The whaling vessels were equipped to boil down the blubber while at sea. The chunks of blubber were hoisted up to the main deck. The small pieces were placed in very big vats or kettles that were hung over a fire on the ship's deck. Then the blubber was boiled down to oil. The oil was stored in large barrels in the hold of the ship. (When the barrels were put on board, they were packaged. The cooper and carpenter assembled the barrels as needed.)

LENGTH OF TRIP

These whaling vessels would be at sea from six months to a couple of years, depending on the size of the ship and their luck in catching whales.

As time went on, ships had to sail further away to get whales. The first sailing ship which sailed into the Pacific Ocean in search of whales is said to be the "Rebecca," which sailed from Dartmouth, September 21, 1783. As the Panama Canal had not yet been dug, the ships had to sail around the Cape of Good Hope or Cape Horn to get to the Pacific Ocean. (Trace their route on the large map or globe in your room.) When the "Rebecca" completed her search, she returned to Dartmouth with a cargo of 750 barrels of sperm oil and 180 barrels of whale oil.

WHALING IN DARTMOUTH

As early as 1755, whaling was pursued by Dartmouth men. We know that four vessels were engaged in whale hunting in 1765. Whaling vessels were built on both the Acushnet and Apponegansett Rivers.

As many as fifty whaling vessels were fitted out annually in Dartmouth from 1770–1775. In this work, more than one thousand men found employment as seamen. Since whaling was then in its infancy, the whalers did not have to go too far off shore to catch whales. The great whales came fairly close to the shore where the settlers lived.

The earliest whaling schooners were smaller than the whalers built later on. When the smaller ships were used, the whale blubber was not boiled down at sea. Instead, the captured whale, or possibly two whales, would be towed into the Acushnet River Harbor. There, the blubber was removed and boiled down to oil in what was called a trypot. This oversized pot, four to six feet in diameter, was located on the shore of the river.

By the time of the Revolutionary War, the number of whaling vessels in Dartmouth had increased to sixty. We have already learned that most of them were destroyed by the English during the war.

In 1785, ten years after the British raid, only one whaling vessel was left in Dartmouth. After that, no other ship left our shores until 1787. Then the townspeople began to renew their interest in whaling and the business again became an important one for our town.

When people think of whaling, they usually think of the city of New Bedford — the offspring of Dartmouth — which like many offspring grew larger than its mother. New Bedford was recognized as the outstanding whaling port in the world. For many years, it was the chief seat of the American whale fishery. With the largest whaling ports next door to us, many Dartmouth men put out to sea on New Bedford whalers. Some Dartmouth men were owners of whale ships that claimed New Bedford as their home port.

But after New Bedford separated itself from Dartmouth in 1789, the present town of Dartmouth continued to do some whaling — although on a much smaller scale than New Bedford. Records show that five Dartmouth vessels were engaged in whale fishery in the year 1837. At the same time, 129 Dartmouth men were employed in whaling.

When whaling was at its peak around 1845, Dartmouth had as many as one dozen vessels in the fleet of whalers. In 1873, Dartmouth had three vessels with seventy-five men engaged in whale fishing. At that period, whale oil was used in lamps.

The whaling business declined rapidly after the discovery of petroleum (oil). The obtaining of petroleum was less risky and dangerous than chasing whales. Besides, petroleum provided a better grade of oil for lighting purposes. But while whaling lasted, it added color to our way of life.

Presently, whaling is carried on by huge ships. Whales are spotted by airplanes. Then powerboats leave the huge ship and catch the whale. If whales continue to be hunted this way, they undoubtedly will become extinct.

DARTMOUTH WHALERS

The following is a list of some of the whalers built in Dartmouth by Matthews, Mashow, and Company between 1845 and 1858:

Bark Benjamin Cumminns
Bark Cape Horn Pigeon
Bark Henry H. Crapo
Bark Morning Light
Bark Morning Star
Bark Sea Queen
Bark Tropic Bird
Brig China
Brig Norma
Schooner John Mashow
Schooner J.W. Flanders
Schooner Mosell
Schooner Ocean Queen
Schooner Pearl

Here are two poems about whaling written by seventh graders at the Mary Crapo School in 1959–1960. They are good!

A WHALE OF A TALE

Here's a whale of a tale, me hearties!
A whale of a tale, it's true.
But you'd be saying the very same thing
If it suddenly happened to you.
We set sail on Friday morning
Out on the ocean wide.
Friday it be an unlucky day
And the skipper's wife, she cried,
"Oh, please! Don't leave Old Dartmouth Town!
Please be home today!
Once you're on those open seas
Then you are gone to stay!"

Once we were out upon the sea
The skipper saw a whale.
Too late! The beast rose up on high
And struck us with its tail.

There's an old saying 'mongst sailors
"A dead whale or a stove-in boat"
And our good hulk Esmerelda
Was ne'er more seen afloat.

I am the only sailor left
Who remembers that fateful time
And if it were not a whale of a tale
I would not have set it to rhyme.

—Gina L Sherman

WHALES

There are many kinds of whales
Sulphur-bottoms, right ones
None with fins and all with tails
Black and even white ones
Famous one like Moby Dick
And when they're ill, like this
A gritty substance, when they're sick
Turns into ambergris.

They swim and sail the ocean wide
And oh boy! Would you rave
If you could see a whale inside
It looks just like a cave.
Whales guzzle up their dinners
And really get quite fat
There's plenty of blubber for skinners
So what do you think of that?

—Carol Portnoy

A whale smashing a boat with his powerful tail (flukes).

CHAPTER 14

THE MILLS OF DARTMOUTH

Some of you live in Russells Mills or Smith Mills. Did you ever stop to think of how these sections of Dartmouth got their names? This story will give you the answer.

EARLY SETTLERS

The earliest settlers had a full-time job getting food, clothing, and shelter. There was little or no time for leisure. Eventually, as the population began to increase, people began to think of how much easier a settler's task would be if he could take his trees to a sawmill to be cut into lumber (boards) for home building and other purposes. People also sought a quicker way to grind corn and wheat into corn meal and flour. (The man who did this work was called a miller.)

There were many streams in Old Dartmouth. Waterpower and wind were the only power the colonists could control and use. Therefore, settlers gathered near the area of water, especially at Smith Mills and Russells Mills. Wherever water was available, the settlers began to use it for waterpower. The names Russells Mills and Smith Mills clearly indicate that mills were established in both places.

Unfortunately, some records about Dartmouth's early history have been destroyed. Therefore, we are unable to tell the complete story of the town's infancy since little information is available.

SMITH MILLS

In the year the town was incorporated, 1664, two men, Henry Tucker and George Babcock, were given permission to build a mill at what is now Smith Mills. We don't know just when the mill was completed, but we know it was built before 1681. How can we be sure of that? Because town meeting records of Dartmouth for 1681 were to be posted at "the mills." (Notice the plural is used indicating there must have been more than one mill.) The Paskamansett River supplied the power for the mills.

Town records prove that there was a gristmill and a fulling mill for weaving cloth in Smith Mills in 1702. The fulling mill was in operation until 1775. How many years is that?

How did Smith Mills get its name? In 1706, Elishib Smith bought the mill site in Smith Mills. He built a sawmill. There was a need for a sawmill, for much of North Dartmouth was still heavily wooded. Elishib and his family controlled the mills in Smith Mills for close to a century. Smith Mills was named for these mill-owning Smiths.

Benjamin Cummings bought out the Smith property in 1792. He, too, built a sawmill. Later a cotton factory was erected nearby. In 1821, "The Mercury," an early New Bedford newspaper, carried an advertisement seeking a man to run the cotton mill in Smith Mills. The 1801 records refer to an "oil mill." When the Cummings property was sold in 1823, it was sold with "oil mill and blacksmith shop."

Every colonial town had a blacksmith. The blacksmith made iron shoes for horses and oxen. He also made nails, tools, and iron pots.

In the year 1899, Smith Mills had a gristmill, a sawmill, two blacksmith shops, and two wheelwright shops. (The wheelwright made wooden wheels, wagons, carts, and spinning wheels.)

HIXVILLE

The Hixville section of North Dartmouth also had a mill. About one mile east of Hixville Center, on the road to Faunce Corner, the road crosses the Noquochoke River. This was the site of a mill which in 1710 was called a "new saw mill." Probably many cedar and pine trees of North Dartmouth were made into lumber there. An 1899 "History of Bristol County" states that at that time Hixville had a sawmill and a blacksmith shop.

In 1768, a mill was located south of Smith Mills on Chase Road near the junction of the road from Cedar Dell. The mill was known as Barker Mill.

PADANARAM

We know there was a sawmill in Padanaram in the early seventeen hundreds because in 1708 the townspeople voted to "lay out a highway near Ponaganset sawmill." Another sawmill began to operate in Padanaram around 1776. It was in operation for thirty years. A rich trader, John Wady, purchased a farm at the head of the Apponegansett River where the Apponegansett River and the brook meet. (The brook is described as Allen's or Howland's Brook) "on which yoused to stand a saw mill." Records in 1780 show that Mr. Wady owned two mills, but only the sawmill is mentioned by name.

Shortly after 1800, a windmill was erected in Padanaram at the corner of Middle and School Streets. The wind served as power for a mill. This mill was a gristmill.

RUSSELLS MILLS

At least a dozen mills were located at Russells Mills at one time or another. Most of them were on the Paskamansett River which flows in back of the present-day firehouse. Other mills were located on Destruction Brook. Destruction Brook joins the Paskamansett River a short distance below Russells Mills Village (Davoll's Store). Both flow into Slocum River.

How did Russells Mills get its name? It was named for an early Dartmouth settler, Joseph Russell. He and his family owned and operated mills here for several generations. How long is a generation?

Early in the town's history, Russells Mills had a gristmill. As early as 1702, a fulling mill was located at Russells Mills. Records show that Potomska Road (it leads from Little River Road to Rock-o-Dundee Road) was laid out in 1702. The records indicate that this road passed over the river, where Joseph Russell's fulling mill was located. This mill changed hands several times before being acquired by Benjamin Cummings. He decided to change the mill from a fulling mill to a shingle mill. What a big help that was for the earliest settlers who were hewing

Old Grist Mill in Russells Mills

shingles by hand. That was one of their jobs during the long winter months. They sold the shingles they didn't need.

There was also a carding mill located at Russells Mills. It was probably started about 1830. It was in operation until 1860. Perhaps you are wondering what work was done at a carding mill. At a carding mill, sheep's wool was cleaned and combed. Then it was formed into rolls about twelve inches long. The process after this was called spinning. Most of the spinning was done in the homes by the women. Research tells us there was only one carding mill in Dartmouth in 1873.

Giles Slocum established an iron forge in Russells Mills in 1787.

The "Medley" (New Bedford's first newspaper) carried this advertisement in 1794: "Joseph and Elihu Russell of Dartmouth offer to 'dress and colour cloth at their new works at Russells Mills.' " According to an 1873 Gazetteer, in that year, there were five or six sawmills in the town. The lumber for the mills turned out lumber in the form of lathes, clapboards, and shingles. These were used for buildings.

Records of 1899 indicate that at that time Russells Mills had a gristmill (Allen and Howland Mill), a sawmill, a blacksmith shop, and a wheelwright shop.

For many years there was a vacant mill standing in Russells Mills not far from the village. It was a gristmill that had been in operation as late as the 1950s.

Wouldn't it be fun to visit one of Dartmouth's old mills! Which one would you most like to see? Why?

CHAPTER 15

THE WHITTLING YANKEE

Have you a nickname? What is it? Who gave it to you? Does it suit you? What nickname is often used for Dartmouth High School athletic teams? Is it a good one for them?

Read this story about a Dartmouth man whose nickname was an apt one for him.

BOYHOOD DREAM

What do we mean when we say a person is a "native" of Dartmouth? Are you a native of Dartmouth?

The inventor of the plow was a Dartmouth native. His name was Jethro Wood. Jethro Wood was born in Dartmouth in the year 1774. Like many of the early Dartmouth residents, his parents were Quakers.

Most boys like to tinker with things. Jethro Wood was no exception. As a child, Jethro dreamed of making a plow that would be an improvement on the wooden plow used for centuries. One day the youth took a pewter cup and melted it. From this, he moulded a toy model (miniature) plow. Next, he made a small harness. You would probably never guess what he used for the harness. He cut the buckles off a pair of braces. Today we call braces, suspenders.

What do you suppose Jethro did next? He caught the family cat and fastened her to the plow. Then he drove her through his mother's flower garden. He thought it was fun to have the cat pull the plow, but his mother was very displeased when she saw what had happened to her flower garden. She liked her flowers very much and did not appreciate the results of Jethro's experiment with his cat and plow. Besides, she took pity on the poor cat! That was the last time Jethro used the cat as a beast of burden.

Jethro may have stopped annoying the cat, but he kept right on trying to improve the plow.

WOOD'S NICKNAME

Later Jethro moved from Massachusetts to New York. There people called him "the Whittling Yankee." Let's see why they gave Wood that nickname.

Do you know what whittling is? As a boy, your father may have done some whittling. Many boys like to whittle. In colonial days in our country, the men spent long winter evenings whittling with their jack knives. They whittled out wooden bowls, plates, and spoons. They whittled out other things too, including spindles for the spinning wheel.

Almost every boy was the proud owner of a good knife, which he kept sharp. With this he made his own toys, such as tops, whistles, bows and arrows, or sometimes even a wooden doll for his sister. Wooden dolls were very popular in early America.

Jethro Wood whittled day after day. This explains how Wood got the nickname "Whittling Yankee." He was determined and convinced he was going to make a better plow. That's why he did so much whittling. For his first trials, Jethro used a potato — a long potato rather than a round potato. He cut away (whittled) small pieces of the potato until he had the curve he thought he wanted for a plow. Using this as a pattern, he fashioned a plow out of iron.

A "Yankee" is a person who lives in the northeast section of our country. We know that Dartmouth is in Massachusetts. We also know that Dartmouth is in the northeast section of the United States. Therefore, we can be spoken of as "Yankees." Now can you understand how Wood got his nickname? How well deserved was the nickname by which Wood became known?

THOMAS JEFFERSON'S INTEREST

Wood patiently worked on his plow for many years. At the same time, Thomas Jefferson, the third president of the United States, was also trying to invent a new plow. Of course, as president, Thomas Jefferson kept very busy running the affairs of the United States. Even though his spare time was limited,

Jefferson made some improvements on the plow. He used a sheet of thin iron along the edges of his wooden plow. The iron made the plow stronger and it could stand rougher usage than the all-wooden plow.

Jefferson learned that Wood was also working to improve the plow. Jefferson wrote several letters to Wood urging him to keep trying until he achieved his goal. Thomas Jefferson's letters very much encouraged Jethro Wood.

SUCCESS

Jethro, much encouraged by President Jefferson's interest, kept on trying to make a better plow to use in the fields. Finally, in 1819, after many years of effort, his dream came true. He succeeded in making a better type plow. Indeed, he received a patent on his invention — a patent that was renewed in 1833 principally because of the support and concern in the United States Congress of two very well known Americans, Daniel Webster, the famous orator from Massachusetts, and William H. Seward, who is famous chiefly because of the purchase of Alaska in 1867.

What was different about Wood's plow? To begin with, Jethro Wood's plan was for a cast iron plow, not an all-wooden plow. Jethro's plow was all iron except for the handles and beam. In addition, it had replaceable parts. That meant if one part of the plow became worn or was broken, a farmer did not have to buy a whole new plow. He could send to Jethro Wood's shop and buy just the part he needed. Wood's plow became very popular. His iron plow made it easier to till the land.

Wood produced the best mould form for the iron plow of the time. Your mother uses a mould (mold) when she makes jello.

Today's plows, for the most part, still retain the shape designed by Wood.

The use of cast iron in stoves in later years was one of the results of Wood's experimentation.

Do you see how clever this Dartmouth Native, Jethro Wood, was?

CHAPTER 16

THE SALT INDUSTRY

THE IMPORTANCE OF SALT

Did you realize that our bodies require salt? We do not need much salt to be healthy, but we must have some salt. You may be thinking, "I never shake salt on my food before eating it." That may be true, but probably your mother adds salt to your food as she cooks it.

Long before people began to use ice to keep their food from spoiling, they used salt as a preservative. For several reasons, salt was an absolute necessity for the pioneer settlers in this country. The early settlers salted or smoked all kinds of meat and fish. Even animals will find salt springs because they know they need salt for their bodies. The early settlers discovered the salt springs used by the animals. They used them, too.

SALT MAKING

People living on the seashore, like Dartmouth, could get their salt by evaporating the ocean water. In the early 1700s, the salt industry started in Dartmouth. Most of the salt was sold elsewhere. Salt making was as important industry here. Salt works were located along the shores of Smith Neck and Mishaum Point. One section of Dartmouth, Salter's Point, was originally known as "Salthouse Point." Records in 1720 refer to "the road leading to the salt house point." We can never forget that Salter's Point was a salt works area, can we?

In the 1800's salt works were located at Salter's Point, Mishaum Point, Nonquitt, on the Gulf (Hill) Road near Padanaram Bridge, on Bakerville Road, and in Russells Mills. There were also several salt works on both sides of the Apponegansett River in Padanaram.

In 1810, a salt works started at Ricketson's Point, South Dartmouth. In that year, Clark Ricketson leased (rented) to Isaiah

Salt works — Padanaram

Small an area of land "sufficient to contain 80 cranes of salt works." The lease price was set at $26.00 a year.

Records prove that in the year 1840 there were thirteen establishments for the manufacture of salt in Dartmouth.

You may be curious about the amount of salt water required to make one bushel of salt. Approximately three-hundred and sixty gallons of seawater was needed to produce one bushel of salt.

How much did this salt cost? The price varied, but fifty cents a bushel was the highest price paid for the salt.

GETTING THE SALT

You may be wondering just how the salt was taken out of the salt water. Here is a description of one way this was done.

Salt water was pumped from the ocean (Buzzard's Bay). The pumping was done by windmills. We usually think of the Netherlands (Holland) or Cape Cod when we think of windmills. Did you ever imagine that Dartmouth's shores were once dotted with picturesque windmills?

The water was pumped from the sea through pipes made of hollowed logs into shallow vats; the power to do this was supplied by windmills. These vats were shallow wooden trays. They were only about one foot deep. They were not very large, usually about fifteen feet square. At night and in rainy weather, covers were placed over these vats.

Cranes were used to place the covers on the vats because they were bulky and heavy. They were covered at night to prevent the fog or dew from slowing down the process of evaporation. For the same reason, of course, the vats were covered during rainy weather.

The salt water went through four vats before the sun evaporated all the water. The vats were arranged in tiers, or layers, one above the other. There were usually four vats in a tier. The water ran through wooden spouts from the top vat into the next vat and so on until the bottom vat was reached. This usually took about three weeks. By that time, most of the water was dried out of the salt. The finished salt was left. The salt was placed in a salt house to thoroughly dry. The wind, blowing through the open spaces purposely left between the boards in the sides of the salt house, finished drying the salt.

Because the sun was used to evaporate the water, the salt was made in the summer months — usually from May to October when the sun was the hottest.

Why don't you perform an experiment? Fill a dish with salt water and set it on a window sill in your classroom. See how long it takes the water to evaporate. Notice a little salt is left after the water evaporates.

THE BRUSH METHOD

Another method of salt making was the brush method. In the brush method of making salt, water dripped down on small trees or shrubs which held the salt particles. The salt was shaken off afterwards. The water dripped down from one tier to another. It might interest you to learn that the final water was called "bitter water." This bitter water was sold to the Norton Grinding Company in Worcester, Massachusetts, at an excellent price of $1.00 a barrel. The grinding company used the bitter water as a lubricant in shaping and smoothing ironwork.

A couple of centuries ago if your mother was running low on salt, undoubtedly your father would have hitched his oxen or horses to a wagon and driven to the salt house to buy some salt. He might have taken you along with him for the ride. Don't you think it would have been interesting to see the salt works?

Remember, some salt making had been carried on in Dartmouth since the early 1700s. As time passed, it was found we could buy salt very cheaply from the West Indies. (Locate the West Indies on the map.) But at the time of the War of 1812 (when we again fought against England), the English ships so controlled the seas that we could no longer secure salt from the West Indies. This forced us to again make salt.

Saltworks at Ricketson's Point,, Padanaram, So. Dartmouth in the year 1894. This drawing shows only a small section of the salt works. There were many more trays and covers just like the ones you see in this picture.

Dartmouth's older residents may recall seeing the last salt works in Padanaram. The salt works on Gulf Road employed the brush method. The other method was used in the salt works on Smith Neck Road near Gulf Road.

SALT WORKS' REMINDER

Some excellent paintings of the Dartmouth salt works were stored in the old Dartmouth High School. The old Town Hall in Padanaram used to have an interesting painting of the salt works in Dartmouth. Try to see if it still exists in the new Town Hall.

TIDBITS OF INTEREST ABOUT OLD DARTMOUTH

1. Do you know what a ferry is? As early as 1695, a ferry was in operation at the site of the present Hix's Bridge in Westport. Westport was then a part of Dartmouth.

2. Early in our town's history, there were no bridges across the rivers. Those who had to cross the rivers usually used small boats. In some places, they walked across the river at low tide.

Before 1835, there was no bridge across Apponegansett River in Padanaram. However, a person could get across the river by ferry. The ferry was run by Mr. Charles Slocum. The fare was four pence - half penny per passenger.

When the first bridge was built across the Apponegansett River in 1835, it was a toll bridge. That meant you had to pay to use the bridge. The money went to the people who had built the bridge. In this way they got back the money they spent building the bridge. Of course, they also needed money to keep the bridge in good repair.

The tolls may seem strange to you. They were as follows:

1¢ for each sheep or swine (pig)
4¢ for each cattle
4¢ for each foot passenger
8¢ for horse and rider
10¢ for horse and wagon
16¢ for each horse and chaise, chair, sulky, or sleigh
25¢ for each horse and coach, phaeton, or chariot
20¢ for each cart or sled drawn by more than one beast
4¢ for each beast without rider

Since 1870, no charge has been made to cross the Padanaram Bridge. For how many years have people been able to use the bridge without paying tolls?

3. Historians do not feel that the earliest Dartmouth houses had fireplaces. Why do they feel that way? The minutes (records) of 1710 contain this item, "William Soule is Appoynted to procure a Pot to make a fire in and Coals to burn it in."

4. Early in our country's history, there were very few roads. Rivers and streams or the trails made by the Native Americans were the only highways.

However, as soon as people began to use ox-carts and wagons, they needed roads. Usually the road was made by widening and following the old Native American trails.

When were Dartmouth's first roads built? By 1684, our town had begun to consider laying out roads. Later, a surveyor named Benjamin Crane devoted most of the years from 1710–1721 dividing the town of Dartmouth into farms and laying out roads. He suggested that each road be four rods (one rod equals sixteen and one-half feet) in width. After his death, the width of the roads was reduced to two rods. County Street, one of the earliest streets laid out in the Bedford section of Old Dartmouth, was four rods wide. Maybe you would like to find out how wide the street you live on is.

5. Did you ever wonder what doctor the early residents of Dartmouth called when they were very sick? As far as we can find out, the first doctor in Old Dartmouth was Dr. Benjamin Burg who was born in 1708. He died at the early age of forty. Dr. Burg is buried in the present town of Acushnet.

6. Were the residents of the 1700s self-reliant? It appears so. For at a town meeting of 1768, the townspeople were called upon to consider the matter of "Incouraging our own Manufacturers." What does that mean?

7. In 1774, Captain George Claghorn, builder of the famous ship, "Constitution" (often referred to as Old Ironsides), established a shipyard in the Bedford section of Dartmouth. His shipyard was at the junction of present-day North and Second Streets. Captain Claghorn also built the ship "Rebecca." Some

day, plan to see the "Constitution." It is preserved at Charlestown Naval shipyard.

8. The Quakers (Friends) were among the first people opposed to slavery. In 1716, they went on record as being against slavery. By 1785, all Dartmouth Friends had ceased to have slaves.

9. The Quakers' meetinghouse has been on the same site, on the banks of the Paskamansett River on Russells Mills Road since 1699. The present meetinghouse was built in the year of 1790.

10. The first fire engine in Dartmouth (Bedford Village) was purchased by Joseph Rotch in 1772. This engine was made in England. The engine had double pumps but did not carry water. The townspeople were expected to have water buckets in their homes ready for use in case of fire. Everyone was supposed to help. The buckets were passed from one person to another down a line until they reached the fire engine.

A story is told that one man stored beans in his water bucket. When the bucket was needed, he had forgotten he had filled it with beans. Accidentally, he poured the beans into the fire engine. Of course, the pump became clogged and was useless until the beans were removed. Imagine his embarrassment! How upset the firefighters must have been!

11. Have you ever heard of the apprentice system? In his early youth, the great American, Benjamin Franklin, was an apprentice to his brother.

If the boys in your class had been living two hundred years ago, probably many of them would now be serving as apprentices.

An apprentice is a boy learning a trade from a skilled master. The training started when the boy was about ten years old. His parents signed a paper saying the boy would work faithfully from sunrise to sunset for a period of five to seven years. The apprentice received little or no money, but he did get his room and board. Some apprentices also got clothing. Usually they received a suit every few years to be used only on Sundays so they would be presentable for church on the Sabbath.

Sometimes the life of an apprentice was very hard. Some boys even ran away.

The following article appeared in the 1794 "Medley", the first newspaper in this area, and tells of a Dartmouth apprentice who ran away.

"Run-away from the subscriber, the 27th, an indented (indentured) apprentice boy, by the name of Hattle Brayley; sixteen years old — about four feet six inches high — light complexion and short hair. — Had on, when he went away, a short, green outside coat, fustic-colored broadcloth trousers, patched on the knees, with cloth of the same kind and color as his coat, — a good felt hat. Took with him, a good led coloured broadcloth coat — a jacket and breeches — also a seal skin cap.

Whoever will return said Boy shall receive a handsome reward and all charges. All persons are forbid harbouring or trusting him on any account — and Masters of vessels are hereby forewarned against taking him to sea — as they will answer for it at their peril."

Those apprentice boys who weren't interested in learning a trade or were seeking a more adventuresome life frequently ran away and went to sea. I wonder if this was how Hattle Brayley evaded his apprenticeship?

12. The following entry was found in the Town Meeting records dated April 16, 1868: "Voted not to pay the toll of scholars (pupils) as must cross a toll bridge to attend a Public School." Maybe that is one reason why students were absent so often!

13. What did whalemen from this area do with their leisure time? They did beautiful scrimshaw. Scrimshaw is a carving or drawing done — not on paper, but on a sperm whale tooth, a walrus tusk, or perhaps a piece of ivory. What patience was needed to produce scrimshaw! Some of the articles the seamen made were cribbage boards (cribbage is a game) or

wheels to use in cutting cakes and pies. Scrimshaw is a style of art unique to our country. Look for fine displays of scrimshaw when you visit the New Bedford Whaling Museum. You can also see scrimshaw in jewelry shops. Scrimshaw jewelry for both men and women is very popular. Your mother or father may have a piece.

14. A Dartmouth teacher of the late 1800s had this strange experience while boarding around. One family told him he could sleep in the guest room. Just before getting into bed, he blew out his candle. Imagine his surprise to find something under the bedclothes! Most likely, you could never guess what it was. It was a large cheese that had been placed there (where it was dark) so it could age.

15. You often write stories in school, don't you? Years ago, school children wrote stories for their teachers, too. About 1890, a young Dartmouth student, Almy King, wrote this story in class, As you read it, notice what a clear picture she gives of her school. How can you tell she liked it?

"OUR SCHOOLHOUSE"

"Our school is pleasantly situated in Bakerville, on the east side of the road. It is surrounded by a large yard and fence.

Out of the back windows, we can look out at Buzzard's Bay. There are eight windows and each has curtains. It is painted white with green blinds. Inside there is a stove, six blackboards, a clock, a teacher's desk, four charts, and twenty-four desks. It has a belfry and in it a bell which rings at quarter of nine in the morning to warn the children who are on their way to school that they will be late unless they hurry. It rings again at nine o'clock when school begins. It is the duty of certain boys to ring the bell by means of a heavy rope. Sometimes the bell turns upside down. Then the boys must climb into the belfry and right the bell. The schoolhouse is about thirty feet long and twenty-eight feet wide. The woodwork is grained.

It is very pleasant because the sun shines in most of the day."

If you think this girl seems overly enthusiastic about her school, remember two things — one, many girls were not allowed to go to school in those days, and two, there were not as many places for children to go to as there are today.

Now perhaps you might like to write a description of your school or classroom.

16. In the olden days, people used to gather seaweed in the fall. The seaweed was placed against the foundation of the house to keep out the winter cold, snow, and ice.

You can see the early people used the seaweed as a form of insulation against the cold. Indeed, up to a few decades ago, some people whose homes had no cellars still used seaweed.

Incidentally, some varieties of seaweed can be used to make pudding.

17. The Native Americans referred to Nonquitt, off Smith Neck Road, as "Bare-Kneed Rocks."

18. Potomska, near Little River Bridge, South Dartmouth, was sometimes referred to as the "Cow Yards" because cows were shipped out from there. Some people feel Potomska was called the Cow Yards because cows were allowed to roam all over that area.

19. Early Quaker records refer to Smith Mills as Newtown.

20. How long has Dartmouth had a public library? In 1878, a Literary and Social Club was started in South Dartmouth. The purpose of the club was to establish a public library. The Southworth Library in Padanaram was dedicated in 1890. How wonderful that many people realized the value of a good public library more than a century ago!

21. Very early in the town's history, surveyors of timber and plank were chosen. There were also surveyors of hoop staves, shingles, and clapboard. When your great grandparents were young, they may have rolled hoops from barrels for fun.

22. W.W. Crapo, a son of Henry Crapo, (Do you recall he was a prominent Dartmouth educator in the early 1800s?), told an interesting sidelight about a miller of Russells Mills in the 1850s.

"The miller's gristmill work did not always require his attention. In his spare time, he began to make an article needed on the land. The miller made hay rakes for the neighboring farmers. Watching the miller make these hand-made rakes was a favorite pastime of the boys in the village."

23. You would think it strange if you didn't see a large American flag flying on the school grounds when school is in session. Since 1909, by law, every Massachusetts school must fly the American flag. In his 1892–1893 School Report, Superintendent of Schools, Seth Crocker, remarked, "The American flag now waves over many of our village schools and it is hoped that this beautiful emblem … may ere long be seen floating daily above every school-house in our town."

In his 1897–1898 report, Mr. Crocker announced, "Every school now has a flag."

Thanks chiefly to Mr. Crocker, flags were flying at the Dartmouth schools more than a decade before the law requiring all schools to have flags.

24. You have favorite games you enjoy playing at recess time. Some of the games you like to play are jump rope, hopscotch, baseball, and dodge ball.

In the late eighteen hundreds, school children liked to play tag, jack-stones, London Bridge, and drop the handkerchief. How many of these old favorites have you played?

25. During the War of 1812, an American sentry kept watch at the peninsula opposite the Town Landing. This is where the Slocum River meets the Little River, in the area near Little

River Bridge. Why was the area guarded? It was guarded because the British man-of-war "Nimrod" was anchored offshore and patrolled the New Bedford area closely. That made the Dartmouthites feel that the British might try to sail up the Slocum River to do some damage. The townspeople had not forgotten the 1778 British invasion during the Revolutionary War.

26. During the Revolutionary War, Russells Mills Village displayed a liberty pole. What was a liberty pole? A liberty pole was a pole placed in the ground with a colonist's cap on the top of the pole. This cap represented all the villagers and indicated that the settlers were loyal to the colonial cause.

27. About the year 1700, a Native American meetinghouse was located on the side of the road about one mile from Russells Mills Village on Horseneck Road, South Dartmouth.

28. Nonquitt roads have Native American names. We read about these in our country's and Dartmouth's history; names such as: Samoset, Acushnet, Massasoit, Wamsutta, and King Philip.

29. Gosnold Road in Salter's Point is named in honor of the early explorer, Bartholomew Gosnold.

30. In 1871, the town had a high school and 23 district schools. A sum of $4500 was appropriated for the support of the schools.

31. Research (1871) says, "The people are hardy, industrious, and hospitable. A public library and Lyceum are needed also better railroad accommodations."

32. In 1761, a visitor to Dartmouth, Rev. Paul Coffin, remarked, "This day rode to Dartmouth a spacious town. Twenty miles will carry you through it. Rocks are all over the whole town."

POPULATION

1675 — about 30 homes
1776 — 6,773 inhabitants

(These figures were for Old Dartmouth, which also included New Bedford, Fairhaven, Acushnet, and Westport.
These towns were not set off from Dartmouth until 1787.)

1790 — 2,499
1800 — 2,660
1810 — 3,219
1820 — 3,636
1830 — 3,866
1840 — 4,135
1850 — 3,868
1860 — 3,883
1870 — 3,367
1880 — 3,430
1890 — 3,122
1900 — 3,669
1910 — 4,378
1920 — 6,493
1930 — 9,000
1940 — 9,011
1950 —11,115
1960 —14,608
1970 —19,132
1980 —23,768
1990 —27,269
2000 —29,074
2010 —35,491

BIBLIOGRAPHY

1. Barber, John — Historical Collection's Relating to the History and Antiquities of Every Town in Massachusetts (1841)

2. Board of Trade — New Bedford, Massachusetts, Its History, Industries, Institutions, and Attractions (1899)

3. Borden, Alanson — Bristol County, Massachusetts (1899)

4. Boston Historical Co. — Our Country and Its People (1899)

5. Bradford, William — Bradford's History of Plimouth Plantation (reprint from the original manuscript) (1898)

6. Comiskey, Kathleen R. — History of Education in Dartmouth (unpublished thesis) (1954)

7. Ellis, Leonard B. — History of New Bedford and Its Vicinity (1892)

8. Fisbe, John — Beginnings of New England, Houghton, Mifflin & Co. Boston (1889)

9. Flagg, Charles — A guide to Massachusetts Local History (1907)

10. Harris, Sheldon H. — Paul Cuffee, Black American and the African Return

11. Heath, Dwight (Editor) — Mourt's Relations (1963)

12. Howe, Henry F. — Salt Rivers of the Massachusetts Shore (1951)

13. Howland, Captain Franklin — History of Acushnet (1903)

14. Hurd, Hamilton — History of Bristol County, Massachusetts (1883)

15. Hutt, Frank — History of Bristol County, Massachusetts, Volume I (1924)

16. Johnston, Johanna — Paul Cuffee, America's First Black Captain (1970)

17. Mayhew, Experience — Narratives of the Lives of Pious Indian Chiefs, Women, and Children (1727)

18. Nason, Rev. Elias — A Gazetteer of the State of Massachusetts (1874)

19. Ricketson, Daniel — History of New Bedford and Its Vicinity (1858)

20. Rowlandson, Mary — Narrative of Captivity and Removes (1676)

21. Salvador, George — A Black Quaker (1969)

22. Starbuck, Alexander — History of the American Whale Fishery from Its Earliest Inception to the Year 1876 (1878)

23. Sylvester, Herbert — Indian Wars of New England, Volume I (1910)

24. Waldmer, B. — A Popular History of American Inventions, Charles Scribner's Sons, New York (1924)

MISCELLANEOUS

Old Dartmouth Historical Sketches (1–48)

Dartmouth School Committee Minutes (1839–1922)

Dartmouth School Committee Reports (1852–1853, 1856–1857, 1865–1866, 1870, 1874, 1955–1975, 2010)

Dartmouth Town Meeting Records (1664–1925)

A harpooner ready to strike a whale.